Your
Horoscope
2020

....

Virgo

D0424067

Your
Horoscope
2020

....

Virgo

24th August - 23rd September

igloobooks

igloobooks

Published in 2019
by Igloo Books Ltd
Cottage Farm
Sywell
NN6 0BJ
www.igloobooks.com

0819 001.01
2 4 6 8 10 9 7 5 3 1
ISBN 978-1-78905-720-1

Written by Belinda Campbell and Denise Evans

Cover design by Dave Chapman
Edited by Bobby Newlyn-Jones

Printed and manufactured in China

CONTENTS
. . . .

INTRODUCTION
· · · · · · · · · · · · · · · · ·

This horoscope has been specifically created to allow
you to get the most from astrological patterns and
the way they have a bearing on not only your zodiac
sign, but nuances within it. Using the diary section
of the book you can read about the influences and
possibilities of each and every day of the year. It will
be possible for you to see when you are likely to be
cheerful and happy or those times when your nature
is in retreat and you will be more circumspect. The
diary will help to give you a feel for the specific
'cycles' of astrology and the way they can subtly
change your day-to-day life.

THE CHARACTER OF THE VIRGIN

·················

As kind as they are critical, as down to earth as they are successful, Virgoans are the perfectionists of the zodiac. They set ideals for everyone, themselves included, to strive towards. Ruled by Mercury, the planet of communication, they will happily offer their opinions on any given subject, both when asked to and when not. Whilst communicating is a forte for many Virgoans, their sharp tongues and analytical brains can mean that their opinions sometimes come across as being overly critical. Extremely detail-orientated, and with the highest of standards, others can seem to fall short by comparison. However, any criticism Virgoans offer will usually be constructive and full of good intentions.

In opposition to neighbouring Leo, the sign of Virgo belongs to the sixth house, which focuses on health and service. Others often look to Virgoans for help and guidance about dieting or big decisions because they know that they will receive practical, informative and candid advice. Virgoans may well be nicknamed 'Dr Phil' (also a Virgoan!) in their group of friends. As well as giving second-to-none counsel, Virgoans are efficient, resourceful and have exceptional attention to detail. Such strong attributes can help Virgoans to become the highest of achievers, but their humility means they are unlikely to let any success go to their heads. Virgoan superstar Beyoncé, for example, is known for her humble attitude despite her incredible accomplishments and global fame. Symbolised by a Virgin, modest and sometimes shy Virgoans will remain as well presented and orderly as their daily to-do lists. They do not usually opt for anything too showy, as is their more introverted, negative way. Born at the end of summer when the leaves begin to transform in colour, Virgoans are a unique combination of certainty, control and change, which allows them to be both organised and organic.

THE VIRGIN

Not to be taken too literally, the symbolic sign of the Virgin represents many qualities in good, yet sometimes naïve, Virgoans. Astraea, the Greek goddess of justice and innocence, makes up the Virgo constellation and is often depicted as the Virgin symbol. However many compliments Virgoans may receive, they will likely remain modest and could come across as shy, giving them an air of innocence that can be highly attractive. This purity can by why they are often seen as being very prim and proper to the outside world, but their qualities are measured best by their ability to always find the good. Virgoans tend to be fair and true thanks to their methodical ability to weigh up the facts with intelligence and honesty, much like Librans. Demeter, the Greek goddess of harvesting, is another deity associated with the Virgin symbol. Holding a sheaf of wheat, Demeter is the mother of Earth's fertility and the reason we have seasons, which is perhaps why mutable Virgoans – with their foresight and love of planning – can make wonderful agriculturists.

MERCURY

The speed at which some analytical Virgoans process information is surely inherited from their ruling planet of Mercury, which orbits the Sun faster than any other planet in the solar system. Mercury is named after the Roman god of the same name, who is typically shown with wings on his head and feet. Virgoans are similarly quick, especially when it comes to thinking. However, the speed at which thoughts race around their heads can mean they sometimes overthink things and obsess over the smallest of details. This can make them hold a grudge better than most. 'Mercury in retrograde' is a phrase that is often met with fearful faces, but what does it mean? Three times a year, Mercury seemingly begins to move backwards and is blamed for many communication, media, technology and travel failures. Whilst many people might avoid making big decisions, signing important documents or arranging trips during a retrograde, ever-practical Virgoans will probably not let their ruling planet slow them down in any significant way.

ELEMENTS, MODES AND POLARITIES

Each sign is made up of a unique combination of three defining groups: elements, modes and polarities. Each of these defining parts can manifest in good and bad ways, and none should be seen to be a positive or a negative – including the polarities! Just like a jigsaw puzzle, piecing these groups together can help illuminate why each sign has certain characteristics and help us find a balance.

ELEMENTS

Fire: Dynamic and adventurous, signs with Fire in them can be extroverted. Others are naturally drawn to them because of the positive light they give off, as well as their high levels of energy and confidence.

Earth: Signs with the Earth element are steady and driven with their ambitions. They make for a solid friend, parent or partner due to their grounded influence and nurturing nature.

Air: The invisible element that influences each of the other elements significantly, Air signs will provide much-needed perspective to others with their fair thinking, verbal skills and key ideas.

Water: Warm in the shallows and freezing as ice. This mysterious element is essential to the growth of everything around it, through its emotional depth and empathy.

MODES

Cardinal: Pioneers of the calendar, cardinal signs jump-start each season and are the energetic go-getters.

Fixed: Marking the middle of the calendar, fixed signs firmly denote and value steadiness and reliability.

Mutable: As the seasons end, the mutable signs adapt and give themselves over gladly to the promise of change.

POLARITIES

Positive: Typically extroverted, positive signs take physical action and embrace outside stimulus in their life.

Negative: Usually introverted, negative signs value emotional development and experiencing life from the inside out.

VIRGO IN BRIEF

The table below shows the key attributes of Virgo.
Use it for quick reference and to understand more about
this fascinating sign.

SYMBOL	RULING PLANET	MODE	ELEMENT	HOUSE
The Virgin	Mercury	Mutable	Earth	Eighth

COLOUR	BODY PART	POLARITY	GENDER	POLAR SIGN
Yellow, Orange	Stomach, Intestines	Negative	Feminine	Pisces

LOVE

Virgoans can be choosey lovers. They are not ones
to frequently fall in love, but their devotion can last
an eternity when finally bestowed on a worthy soul.
Anyone chosen by these notoriously picky characters
should feel very special indeed. Virgoans can have a
tendency to find faults or nitpick about trivial matters,
which can be troublesome in love. Wanting to tweak or
change minor issues may seem harmless and necessary
to mutable Virgoans, but celebrating the differences in
their relationships will prove to be far more rewarding
than finding flaws. This optimistic outlook of finding the
positive needs to extend to themselves too, as they are
too often left confused as to what their partners see
in them.

Although symbolised by the Virgin, Virgoans are not
always naïve when it comes to their relationships. They
present themselves impeccably to the outside world with
lint rollers at the ready, but they can also be extremely
laidback when they feel at ease in a relationship.
When they find themselves in the arms of true love,
they will no longer worry about their hair being out
of place or their clothes being creased. Curious with
a mutable nature, Virgoans are often open to trying
new things, which can help keep any long-term flames
of love burning brightly. They may struggle initially
with exposing themselves to vulnerability, resulting in
them not always giving their love freely. However, when
Virgoans choose to lower their emotional barriers their
endless affection can be well worth the wait.

With a deeply rooted Earth element, Virgoans will most appreciate partners who enjoy getting outside and who understand the importance of protecting the planet. Eco-conscious and organised, finding someone who will go trekking in the countryside can be just as important to Virgoans as finding a partner who takes the time to separate the plastic and glass for recycling. Chores aside, they will be the most charmed by someone who brings fun and energy into their meticulously planned lives.

ARIES: COMPATIBILITY 3/5

There's not a lot that's similar about how an Arian and Virgoan think and approach their daily decisions. The Arian rushes in excitedly to almost everything, whereas the Virgoan needs to exhaust all the facts and options first. The Arian can teach the Virgoan the benefits of not getting too bogged down with decisions, and the Virgoan can teach the Arian the equal importance of noticing the smaller details in life. When these two team up, they will understand that they are very, very different, and will likely admire those differences in one another.

TAURUS: COMPATIBILITY 3/5

A Taurean and Virgoan can make for a real power couple. The Taurean's dogged approach to fulfilling goals and the Virgoan's practical and busy mind will see this pair securing a successful future together. The Virgoan can appear overly critical and may end up hurting the Bull's feelings unintentionally. Ruled by Mercury, the planet of communication, the Virgoan can be very attuned to the Taurean's needs and will try to fix any problems within the relationship. These two will likely share many things in common and can form a lifelong companionship, even if a whirlwind romance isn't in the stars.

GEMINI: COMPATIBILITY 1/5

A Virgoan may initially be attracted to a Geminian's charm and wit, but is likely to soon feel irritated by the flights of fancy. The steady Virgoan can feel too reserved for the Geminian, and the fast-paced Geminian can be too unpredictable for the Virgoan. Both ruled by Mercury and strong believers in communication, these otherwise contrasting characters may end up feeling as if they are speaking two completely different languages. However, their mutual love of change and talent for adaptability may well be what makes this relationship last longer than predicted.

CANCER: COMPATIBILITY 3/5

A practical-minded Virgoan could be the balancing force that a Cancerian needs in a partner. The Virgoan will feel loved and protected by the nurturing Cancerian, but by contrast the Cancerian can at times feel hurt by the naturally critical Virgoan. Thanks to ruling planet Mercury, the Virgoan's strong communication skills should help them patch up any problems. The Earth element in Virgo and the cardinal influence in Cancer can make for a driven couple, so any loving ambitions that these two share will likely be realised together.

LEO: COMPATIBILITY 2/5

The love of a Leonian can take a Virgoan by surprise;
which isn't something the introverted Virgoan is always
keen on. The clear differences between the studious
Virgoan and show-stopping Leonian can mean that
these two might be quick to write each other off as
potential partners at first glance. The relationship
between this Fire and Earth couple can be a slow
burner, but their slow and steady approach could
well end up with these two winning the race hand in
hand. This couple's strengths are their differences,
and these two hard workers can make for a solid and
complementary couple.

VIRGO: COMPATIBILITY 4/5

If a Virgoan wrote a list, which is highly probable, of
what an ideal partner would consist of, then a fellow
Virgoan would surely tick a lot of those boxes. Detail-
orientated, practical, health conscious, tick, tick, tick!
Here are two planners that will have their wedding date
set and booked in a snap thanks to their impeccable
teamwork. These two high-reaching individuals are a
seemingly perfect couple, from their flawless wardrobes
to their regular date nights. This is an orderly and highly
compatible match, but it can sometimes lack some
spontaneity.

LIBRA: COMPATIBILITY 3/5

Both advocates of diplomacy and justice, a Libran and
Virgoan's love should be fair and true. If these two make any

vows together, they will take them very seriously. However, it is not all contracts and scales in this relationship, as the Mercury-inspired Virgoan and Venus-ruled Libran could both have a shared love of beauty and crafts. A date night at a gallery or the theatre could be perfect for the art-loving Virgoan and Libran couple. The Libran will have plenty of ideas, and the practical Virgoan could be the one that helps make those fancies a reality.

SCORPIO: COMPATIBILITY 5/5

Positioned two places apart on the zodiac calendar, the passionate and loyal bond between a Virgin and Scorpian is a special one. The orderly Virgoan will value the steadiness of the fixed Scorpian, and similarly the loyal Scorpian will appreciate the faithfulness that the Virgoan is known for. With their complementary elements of Water and Earth and their matching negative energies, this typically introverted couple will enjoy the nourishing effects of spending quality time together. Theirs is an intimate relationship but not without some passionate arguments, thanks to the Scorpian's power-ruled influence of Pluto and the Virgoan's sharp tongue.

SAGITTARIUS: COMPATIBILITY 2/5

These two lovers may really have their work cut out for them. Whilst the outdoorsy Sagittarian and Earthy Virgoan both have a strong love for being outside in nature, they have some serious core differences. The Virgoan, for example, loves routine, which the

Sagittarian can't abide. Elsewhere, the wild Sagittarian, who gallops heart first towards goals, can sometimes feel too reckless for the overthinking Virgoan, whilst the Sagittarian might find the Virgoan's overactive mind to be a hindrance. If they can find some common ground, this mutable pair could experience an honest and thought-provoking relationship.

CAPRICORN: COMPATIBILITY 4/5

When a hardworking Capricornian and meticulous Virgoan fall in love, there won't be many cracks in their relationship. With the Virgoan's tool kit of practical skills and the Capricornian's portfolio of material achievements, this hard-working couple may well be best at taking on grand projects. Perhaps building their own home somewhere in the countryside would suit this couple, where their shared Earth element can be appreciated at its best, and their quieter negative energies embraced. This firm relationship may lack some spontaneity, so thoughtful surprises now and again could help keep the excitement alive.

AQUARIUS: COMPATIBILITY 2/5

An idealist Aquarian and realist Virgoan may not be an obvious match, but this couple can be very happy if they find key ideas and goals to share. The organised Virgoan will appreciate the Saturn-ruled part of the Aquarian that represents structure and order, but less so the rebellious Uranus side that enjoys throwing out the rulebook. The Airy Aquarian and Mercury-ruled Virgoan are both freethinkers and should be good at allowing one another room to breathe in the relationship, which both will value. Ultimately, the optimistic Aquarian and the pragmatic Virgoan will need to find a shared ambition to balance out their stark differences.

PISCES: COMPATIBILITY 5/5

Opposites on the zodiac calendar, a hands-on Virgoan and mystical Piscean make a loving match, yet life will not be without the occasional struggle. Water and Earth are elements that can create beautiful things together, but in this couple the emotional Piscean and rational Virgoan could be a tricky balancing act. For example, the Piscean sometimes exhibits an elusiveness that can be attractive or frustrating to the steady Virgoan. Overall, however, these two are deep souls that can empathise and support one another probably better than any other match, and can happily and devotedly serve one another for endless days.

FAMILY AND FRIENDS

It's hard to ruffle unflappable Virgoans, which makes them go-to confidants in times of crisis. Their wise words can be second to none thanks to their honesty and practicality, so offering advice to friends and family is a common practice. Whilst the advice of Virgoans will usually be actively sought, their candid tones can sound callous at times. Even if their intentions are pure, their sharp words can penetrate even the thickest of skins. Virgoans might think that their Cancerian and Scorpian friends have hard shells that can withstand straight talking, for example, but they will actually need to tread lightly because both can be extremely sensitive. After a time, even the most patient of people, such as Taureans, might tire of the Virgoan disapproving tone. To avoid alienating their loved ones, particularly their own children, Virgoans should try to always be constructive rather than overly critical, and give any words of advice without condemnation.

Virgoans' homes most likely reflect their impeccable taste. Their style may be minimal, but it will always be warm. They usually function best if their homes are uncluttered, so if their bedroom is looking disorderly it might be an indication that their thoughts are too. Virgoans can often have a gift for cultivating their Earth element, so a house with a garden could be an important feature, whether it's to grow their own organic vegetables or prize-winning roses. Outdoor space or not, Virgoans might decide to bring the outdoors in and decorate every room with plants that will all have been carefully selected to clean polluted air or thrive on sunny window sills.

Not ones for openly displaying their emotions, Virgoans are more likely to silently sulk until their mood passes. Despite holding stubborn grudges that sometimes feel like a life sentence, Virgoans do forgive and forget with time – as their patient and understanding family and friends will know. Learning to move past bad feeling is essential for Virgoans, as the weight of grievances can start to feel heavy after a while. Opening up to loved ones about how they feel, and letting go of any concerns about vulnerability can be an important first step towards mending any broken bonds and forging stronger friendships. Opposites on the zodiac calendar, Pisceans may well be the emotional key to unlocking the deeper feelings lingering inside of Virgoans.

The social circle of selective Virgoans may be small but strong with lifelong friendships. Whilst they love structure, they suit easy-going and energetic signs that challenge and inspire them. Creative Arians can be the best of friends to crafty Virgoans, and their balance of negative and positive energies are a complementary force that makes for a pioneering and practical alliance.

MONEY AND CAREERS

. . . .

Being a particular star sign will not dictate certain types of career, but it can help identify potential areas for thriving in. Conversely, to succeed in the workplace, it is just as important to understand strengths and weaknesses to achieve career and financial goals.

Thanks to their Earth element, some Virgoans may be attached to material objects, but these hard-working types are usually more driven by goals than they are by money. Whilst these overachievers could be destined to make fortunes by reaching the top of their professions, many are known for their thrifty spending habits. Finding sample sales and scouring the Internet for the best insurance deals, frugal Virgoans will only part with their hard-earned money wisely and are unlikely to go on a shopping splurge. Their tendency to over-analyse could leave them struggling with indecisiveness and considering the pros and cons on almost every purchase. This means plenty of time should be allowed when accompanying them on shopping trips.

MONEY AND CAREERS

Wellbeing is of utmost important to Virgoans, so careers based around healthy living could be worthwhile. One profession that they may thrive in could be as nutritionists or cooks like fellow Virgoan chef, Melissa Hemsley. However, if chopping vegetables doesn't appeal, perhaps the health calling that speaks loudest to analytical and cool-headed Virgoans is within medicine, such as becoming doctors or surgeons. Most Virgoans love to work in a neat and pristine environment, so the clinical order of a hospital could be exactly what the career doctor ordered. Whether it's for the operating table or the dinner table, Virgoans will need a clean and chaos-free workstation if they are to function at their very best.

Virgoans can be meticulous and they often excel at finding fault, so any occupation that involves careful checking and solving problems will be a good fit. Working as consultants may well be something that Virgoans come to later in life, once word of their shrewd observation and effective counsel begins to precede them. Virgoans should be wary of their perfectionist ways when striving for improvement, however, as wanting to check and double-check everything can lead to some projects never being completed. Practical-minded Virgoans could benefit from practising a more relaxed viewpoint that finished is sometimes better than perfect.

As with family, colleagues cannot be chosen. Therefore, it can be advantageous to use star signs to learn about their key characteristics and discover the best ways of working together. Born in the sixth house where service can be second nature, Virgoans often excel at both working for, as well as with, other people. Taureans and Capricornians can work doggedly with hard-working Virgoans through the most difficult of tasks, and will bond over their shared grit and determination. Arians, Leonians and Sagittarians are also potentially good workmates, and could help lighten the load with their positive flames by always encouraging their Virgoan colleagues to down tools and take a break.

HEALTH AND WELLBEING

....

A lack of control can make Virgoans feel anxious, but it is essential that they learn to let go periodically so that they don't make life impossible for themselves and everyone around them. Always ready to give others the best of advice, Virgoans should try to listen to their own wise words. However, seeking external professional advice may also be necessary if their need for control is verging on obsessive. Virgoans notoriously love shopping lists, pros and cons lists and to-do-lists, which can quite literally be endless. Writing down worries might free up some mental space for any overactive minds. Learning to take a break may leave Virgoans pleasantly surprised that the world does not collapse when they enjoy a well-deserved day off.

Virgoans can have a reputation for being negative. In some cases this is just them being practical in their unfiltered candid way, however, sometimes it is a fair assessment and should be mended if it is affecting their happiness. An obvious solution to balance out any negative vibe is to counteract it with some feel-good positivity. Virgoans can become stuck on focusing on the negative and lose sight of the positives surrounding them, but if they take the effort to look around they are likely to be able to find something to be grateful for. It could be family or friends, a good hair day, the sun shining outside, the rain watering the garden, and so on. Spending time with optimistic Sagittarian friends or family members could also be the positive injection that Virgoans need to boost them on a down day.

Virgoans can be incredibly health conscious, and often take extra care of their mental, physical and spiritual health. However, sometimes this can verge on hypochondria. Maybe it's because Virgoans are good at noticing the little things that makes them so alert to their bodily health, but their Internet history is probably littered with online searches desperately trying to self-diagnose the latest potential rash. Scaring themselves with Internet diagnoses is probably a common occurrence, so registering with a local doctor should be the number one priority whenever Virgoans move home. They may well be on a first-name basis before long, but they are always happy to add another name to their Christmas card list. Virgoans generally take such good care of themselves that they should hopefully not have too many reasons to visit the doctor's. Associated with the stomach, Virgoans may wish to take extra care of this area by eating a gut-friendly diet, and easing any anxieties that might be tying their insides into knots.

Virgo

· · · · · · · · · · · · · · ·

2020
DIARY PAGES

JANUARY

. . . .

Wednesday 1st
Happy New Year! You begin 2020 with the Moon in your relationship sector. Spending the opening of the year with someone special will be a great start. You can dream together and drift into worlds only the two of you can enter. If single, you will fall back in love with yourself.

Thursday 2nd
Your creativity and self-expression will get a boost from Mercury, the ideas planet, and Jupiter, who likes to expand everything. This is a great time to brainstorm and make plans as creative projects started now have a high chance of success. Do your research and gather your data.

Friday 3rd
Power and control will be on your mind today, and this could specifically be about the finances you share with another. Mars, the warrior, is at the final degree of your short journeys and communications sector, and is asking you to double-check details before marching on.

Saturday 4th

Family matters can now become entangled with travel and exploration. There can be the formation of solid plans to make holidays or long trips together. You may want to explore cultures that are totally different to your own. Exploring your country of origin will be a good place to start.

Sunday 5th

You have an urge to build foundations now. You can be determined and grounded in your mood. This can also be about digging your heels in and not moving. You may feel stubborn or stuck. However, only you can pick your feet up and move on.

Monday 6th

Advice from teachers and guides, in the form of planets in your creative sector, will come your way and you will take it to heart. This may make you feel restricted or, conversely, empowered. You may dwell on this for the next couple of days, but seek out the lessons it offers.

Tuesday 7th

You may feel unable to express yourself right now, and as if there is a hand over your mouth disabling your power of speech. There is probably a good reason for this. Maybe what you want to say is unhelpful, unkind or simply untrue. Keep quiet for now.

Wednesday 8th

Venus, the planet of love, beauty and harmony, will help you out today, by quietly offering you some sound advice. If you must be a rebel, be a rebel with a cause. Make that cause one that brings harmony. Whatever you have to say today, say it with love.

Thursday 9th

The Moon is in your career sector and you once again feel like speaking your mind. The trouble is, you may be in two minds and not know which one to speak. Be a listener today, gather the facts and information you need and, like a true Virgoan, file it all away.

Friday 10th

It's the first Full Moon of the year, and a lunar eclipse occurs in your social sector. Your friends are also your family and where you feel most nurtured. The Full Moon can highlight this, but the eclipse will bring a shadow. Something does not feel right for you today.

Saturday 11th

Once again, you have lessons to learn. You must stop ignoring them, as they will not be going away any time soon. Uranus, the awakener planet, goes direct today in your travel and exploring sector, so expect some monumental shifts in that area. Feel the tremors and hold tight.

Sunday 12th

Today, you will want to be waited on. You feel lazy and do not want to rise from your slumber. You will want everyone to do your bidding as you dictate what needs doing. Take care not to become obnoxious and alienate your loved ones who like to serve you.

Monday 13th

Those lessons that have been nagging away at you are now staring you in the face. The Sun adds its light and shows you what needs to be learnt regarding creative pursuits, self-expression or children. You may feel like laughing and playing with the Sun here. Work first, play later.

Tuesday 14th

Venus moves into your relationship sector, bringing love and harmony today and for the next few weeks. The Moon in Virgo wants you to explore how you can serve yourself and your partner equally. You care about others, but sometimes you forget about yourself. Health check-ups are best booked now.

Wednesday 15th

Ambition kicks in now and you can methodically plan how to get to the top of a project that you began just after the new year celebrations. You have listened and learnt, and can now put the wheels in motion. Planning and researching make you feel good. Get all your ideas down on paper.

Thursday 16th

The Moon moves into your sector of money and
possessions. You may be torn between wanting to go
on a shopping spree and feeling guilty about spending
money, so decide to stay home and balance the books
instead. Venus makes a good connection to Uranus and
allows you to spend a little.

Friday 17th

Mercury flies into your health and duties sector. He
has many ideas about how you can organise things
better, which is a subject matter close to your heart.
Communicating with others about any mundane
duties will help you to schedule time for you, work and
service to others. A new routine will benefit you.

Saturday 18th

You may be making some short journeys today, and
these could even be inner journeys where you visit
parts of yourself for a short time. Communications with
siblings might reveal behavioural patterns that you
were previously unaware of. This is an intense Moon,
which is likely to bring deep feelings to the surface.

Sunday 19th

Stop and think before you speak today. Mercury and
Uranus are locked in a debate in your duties and
travel sectors. This combination can make for some
arguments, but, on the plus side, it can also provide
innovative ideas about travel and exploration.

Monday 20th

This is quite a lucky day for you, as the Moon is making
good connections between Mars and Venus. You know
what you want and need, and today you will go about
getting it. Love and romance are highlighted for you.
All you have to do is ask.

Tuesday 21st

The Sun is now in your health and duties sector, so this
is a great time to take a good look at anything related
to these areas. You will feel energised and motivated
this month, and you will be able to manage your daily
routines with ease. Starting a new fitness regime will be
beneficial and you are highly likely to stick to it.

Wednesday 22nd

Your heart is yearning to follow creative pursuits, but
work is in the way. You need to use this time to express
yourself, laugh and play. Children can put a smile on
your face today, so get out the crayons and rediscover
your inner child.

Thursday 23rd

Jupiter fills your heart with joy and you can express this easily. Be warned that this can tend to turn you into a rebel. You want to think outside the box and draw attention to yourself. Create some stunning art that gets people wondering.

Friday 24th

A New Moon occurs today in your health and duties sector. You can set late resolutions regarding health, duties and how you serve others. This is not a good day for romance, so you would do best to sit with your diary and reschedule your activities. Organisation is your forte, after all.

Saturday 25th

You have an urge to raise a revolution now. You have itchy feet and want everyone to know about it. You may find yourself leading an expedition somewhere exotic or at least putting it in the planning stages. Social groups are those you can call on for support.

Sunday 26th

The Moon joins your activity party, and you are truly feeling what you are saying. Do you have a soapbox to stand on? You can put your heart and soul into any revolutionary ideas you have now and gather the troops to march onwards. However, do you have time for this?

Monday 27th

Put yesterday's marching boots away and grab your significant other. Today is a day for love and romance. Venus and Neptune add a dreamy essence to the day, while the Moon shines above. This is a typical candlelit-dinner day. Do not waste it.

Tuesday 28th

Stay with the romance of yesterday and drift away into a fantasy land today. You and your partner could make exciting new plans for the future. If you are single, make this a duvet day and watch a favourite film, whilst eating a big tub of ice cream.

Wednesday 29th

You have a need to begin something new now, but something must end first. The Moon is in your sex, death and rebirth sector, which may make you feel as if you are in the planning stages of a great new quest. Be warned, this quest will be deep and intense. Are you ready for this?

Thursday 30th

This is a push-and-pull sort of a day where you will be reviewing the past and thinking of the future. What have you left behind? What skills can you take forwards with you? Where have you been, and where are you now going to?

Friday 31st

You want to move forwards, but past lessons are coming back to haunt you. You may feel guilty about not completing something important now. Issues of power and control surface, and seem to drag you away from your vision. This may be a time to visit a good teacher.

FEBRUARY

. . . .

Saturday 1st

Do you stay, or do you go now? You have a yearning to
get away combined with a yearning for stability. This
makes you restless, as Virgoans do not like indecision.
Curb the urge to be spontaneous today, unless you have
a great new idea to follow through on.

Sunday 2nd

This is a favourable day for love and romance. Giving
yourself permission to do something unusual today
will give you more control about how you spend this
time. Gently coax your partner into joining in. You can
be persuasive in the nicest of ways today. Enjoy getting
what you want.

Monday 3rd

Mercury is asking you to tie up loose ends in your daily
routines. You may have ignored or filed away something
that needs your attention now. Your career is highlighted
and you may feel overloaded or in two minds about a
project. Strengthen your leadership skills and fixate on
one direction for moving forwards.

Tuesday 4th

There will be a lot of talk in your relationships with special people for the next couple of weeks, as Mercury wants to know everything. You may be getting to know someone new and asking a lot of questions. Listening carefully to the answers you are given will aid communication.

Wednesday 5th

Family and career are on your mind now. Who is the boss at home and at work? There will be some aggression around these issues and also possibly some power struggles. Direct communication works best if compassion is used alongside it. Mercury's influence may cause some upset at work today with unchecked words.

Thursday 6th

The Moon in your social sector means that you may feel safe, secure and nurtured by your friendship groups today. These may also be online groups or social media. You will want to have your tribe around you and feel that you are on the same page as everyone else.

Friday 7th

Venus is at the last degree of your love sector, and is asking you to put in a little more effort with special people. If single, then you must use this time to meet your own needs with a little luxury. Power struggles continue and you feel stifled.

Saturday 8th

You can finally begin to connect with your inner spiritual warrior. You will explore sex, death and rebirth with Venus on your side. The Moon makes you feel lazy, but don't feel guilty about wasted time. Use today to rest, play, eat and then sleep.

Sunday 9th

A Full Moon in your dreaming sector shows you how courageous you can be. You can look at dreams and spiritual visions and see what has come to fruition. Where have you dared to be brave and dream beyond your comfort zones? Look back at what you have achieved in the last six months.

Monday 10th

The Moon enters your sign and you will want to check in with yourself. How is your health? Do you need to schedule any check-ups? This is a good time to do what Virgoans do best and go through planners, catch up on filing and tick off to-do lists.

Tuesday 11th

Taking a step back and looking at your daily routines objectively can give you a new perspective. You can sometimes be a martyr and sacrifice yourself for others. Serving others is not the same as giving all you have. Fill up your own vessel today before spreading yourself too thinly.

Wednesday 12th

You can achieve balance today in many ways. Scheduling time for you and time for others will come more easily. Checking your finances and balancing the books will bring satisfaction. You can also bring harmony to the home with a little feng shui.

Thursday 13th

You want to express yourself, but may feel more withdrawn than usual. You do not want to upset the status quo, so are likely to remain silent. Painting, writing or another creative pursuit will help you get this out of your system and restore inner calm. You must make or do today.

Friday 14th

Communication and short travel can be intense now. You may feel that you are running around doing small but necessary chores. Put your best into each one and find the gold in even the most mundane of tasks. Be on the lookout for intriguing conversations that can totally mesmerise you.

Saturday 15th

Mercury is soon to go retrograde in your relationship sector, so you now have a chance to clear up any misunderstandings before they get worse. Double-check any travel arrangements and back up all your devices. Be mindful of your words for the next three weeks.

Sunday 16th

Mars moves into your creativity and self-expression sector, and you will have extra drive and motivation whilst he is there. Your ability for completing artistic projects increases now, and you will find it easy to open up. However, as Mars can be direct and volatile, make sure you use art and not words to show your feelings.

Monday 17th

Mercury retrograde begins. As this happens in your love sector, be sure to communicate with honesty and compassion. Use this time to review and revise anything that has transpired over the last couple of weeks. Put new projects on hold for now and concentrate on what you have already started.

Tuesday 18th

Today, you may find that your dreams take on massive proportions. Neptune is in your love sector, and may add an idealistic edge to your fantasies. You will need to be aware of what is fact and what is purely fiction. There is a danger that you may step too far away from reality.

Wednesday 19th

The Sun now enters your relationship sector and brings
some joy and warmth. It can dissipate any fog that
has been hanging around and enable you to see more
clearly. There will still be dreaminess, but you are more
likely to separate reality from illusion now.

Thursday 20th

The Moon enters your creative sector today, allowing you
to be more authentically artistic. Whatever you create or
are inspired by now may come from deep within you. It
will touch Jupiter (expansion), Saturn (restriction) and
Pluto (transformation). This is a potent recipe for self-
expression so make the most of it.

Friday 21st

Expect the unexpected today, as Mars and Uranus make
a connection in your travel and creative sectors. Mars can
be volatile and Uranus can be disruptive, so this could
result in an unpleasant shock or a welcome surprise. It
could also be something unique and innovative.

Saturday 22nd

The Moon is in your health and duties sector, which may
make you feel drained today. You like to know schedules
and routines, but you may suddenly want to be radical
and go against the norm. Stepping outside the box will
not do any harm, as this is only a passing Moon phase.

Sunday 23rd

Today's New Moon in Pisces is in your relationship sector, which allows you the chance to start over in love and romance. Pisces, the dreamer and empath, asks if you can possibly find empathy for yourself too. Maybe your shadow side needs some attention. Make plans to do some inner work.

Monday 24th

Venus, in your sex, death and rebirth sector, is at odds with Jupiter today. She is not allowed to go deep and wide in these issues for the moment, and must take a break from seeking out secrets and intrigue. Other people's money also features now.

Tuesday 25th

You may feel melancholic today. Your mood will retreat to past times and you will be thinking about how you spent your energy back then. Mars is responsible for this. He is primed for action in your creative sector, but thoughts of the past, and maybe even failures, are holding him back.

Wednesday 26th

Mercury has nothing to say today, and you will feel this like a thick fog in your brain. You will feel mentally drained, which could be a good thing as there is much you want to say but cannot articulate or communicate. Sit tight, this will pass.

Thursday 27th

Are you creating for the love of it or out of duty? You
may have a moment of conscience where your organised
mind suggests that making art or writing poetry is just
a waste of time. You feel more inclined to use up some
physical energy than to be creative today.

Friday 28th

You may have thoughts about building a future
elsewhere in the world, and perhaps want to put down
roots somewhere exotic and learn a new way of life.
Before making any drastic changes, see if you can
content yourself by decorating your home with pieces of
art or furnishings from abroad.

Saturday 29th

Beware of cross words leading to volatile eruptions now.
There could be power struggles and control issues too.
This is not a day to force your will, as you will probably
lose. Your love life is the area in which this is likely to
happen. Cancel that date and stay home.

MARCH

. . . .

Sunday 1st

You feel more at ease about your creative pursuits now.
You can begin to see what you may personally learn
from your creations, as well as how you can transform
something you were not quite happy with. Use this
energy to make some initial plans and jot down ideas.

Monday 2nd

Career takes up most of your attention today. A workplace
that is full of conversation, or just your own internal
dialogue, will do wonders to ground you. Tackling the
fundamental parts of work-based goals will be at the
forefront of your mind.

Tuesday 3rd

What has been building for you at work lately? You
might want to look at how you can climb the corporate
ladder. On the other hand, you might feel safer where
you are. This is a theme for you, but you will find such
indecision grating.

Wednesday 4th

As Mercury's retrograde takes him back into your health and duties sector, you might want to reassess how your daily routines are working out for you. Did you start a fitness class but then stop going? Did you miss a health appointment? Sort this out now.

Thursday 5th

This is a time for friends now. You feel safe within friendship groups, but are you really showing them your true self? Maybe it is time to take off the armour and allow yourself to be vulnerable. Your friends won't bite, and they will more than likely embrace and support your sensitive side.

Friday 6th

Venus is now in your travel and exploration sector, but she is also in Taurus so money and comfort will attach themselves to this area. This could be money spent, so be careful not to throw it all away on the first exciting holiday opportunity that comes your way.

Saturday 7th

The Moon moves into your dream sector today, which may make you become lazy and then feel guilty about it. You tend to be a workaholic and always have something on the go, but you should switch off at these times. Stop feeling bad about it, and award yourself a break.

Sunday 8th

Venus, the planet of love and money, is now sitting right next to Uranus, the disruptor. This is happening in your travel sector, so you may have an excellent idea for how to make a travel plan even more special. You may also find out something regarding love or money.

Monday 9th

Today brings a Full Moon in Virgo, which will illuminate any area regarding yourself as someone who serves others unconditionally. When you are not busy you are a channel for other people, and are highly regarded in this area. Praise is due, and you should accept it graciously.

Tuesday 10th

Mercury goes direct again and will retrace his steps through the end of your health and duties sector, and then into your relationship sector. If you have had any upsets, you can now put them right. It is safe once again to make travel plans and business commitments.

Wednesday 11th

You are preoccupied with getting everything straight today, and that includes money, housework and outstanding jobs. There will be a nagging need over the next two weeks to finish a project, however, you may just want to review whether it is worthy of your time and effort. Think thoroughly before making any final decisions.

Thursday 12th

When the Moon passes through your short journeys and communication sector, as it does today, you can become a detective. You can eke out a confidence from someone or be privy to secrets. People trust you and open up to you at this time. Do not betray their trust. Listen with compassion.

Friday 13th

You will feel very grounded today. Taking walks in nature, doing yoga, meditating or indulging in tasty foods will help you to feel fully in your body. Take advantage of this lovely energy, as your element of Earth will allow you to connect to it more easily.

Saturday 14th

There is a lot of easy energy around today, which may help you relate to a partner and become more intimate. Power struggles will be dropped in favour of making something new from old habits and traditions. Work with your partner on this one.

Sunday 15th

Mercury hits that critical last degree of your health and duties sector today. He is urging you to look at what really needs your attention in this area now. Mercury can think, speak and listen, so use these skills to find out what he is asking you to attend to.

Monday 16th

Mercury comes back into your relationship sector, so there could be some surreal conversations with a loved one at this time. Probing and investigating your partner's deepest emotions comes naturally now. This can also be a chance to explore your shadow side, but beware not to become deluded by false promises.

Tuesday 17th

You will be able to put your heart back into your creative endeavours once more. Speaking your mind, if it comes from the heart, can be fruitful now. You may feel some agitation over the next few weeks and be drawn back to radical behaviours from your past. Look to the future and find a different route.

Wednesday 18th

Your creative sector is packed with some major planetary action this year. Every time the Moon passes, as it does now, you feel emotionally pulled in several directions. There are lessons to be learnt at these times, so sit and listen rather than acting on any feelings.

Thursday 19th

The Moon moves gently into your health and duties sector. Getting a new perspective on your daily routine and fitness will benefit you now. You may find that your routines are boring and not fulfilling you. Revamp your schedule to inject some excitement into it. Think outside the box.

Friday 20th

Here comes the tipping point towards the lighter months. Spring has arrived and the Sun is warming up your sex, death and rebirth sector. This is a great time to set affirmations and intentions for the season. New growth is happening all around and you can be part of that too.

Saturday 21st

The Moon and Mercury are sitting together, which will probably leave you conflicted between matters of the mind and of the heart. Having a conversation between the two can awaken them both. What do you want? What do you really want? You have the drive now to achieve it.

Sunday 22nd

Saturn, the teacher, steps into your health and duties sector today, and will stay here for the next two and a half years. This will present you with some major lessons. Treat Saturn with the greatest of respect and you will pass such lessons with flying colours.

Monday 23rd

Mars, the warrior, and Pluto, the transformer, are together in your creative sector. This may result in a catastrophic event. Something could literally blow up in your face now. Be careful of losing your temper and destroying a piece of art you are not satisfied with. You will regret it.

Tuesday 24th

A New Moon today gives you a second chance to think about the intentions and affirmations you recently considered. These can be for the entire astrological year. You should think of these in terms of shared finances or any project that you wish to bring to a conclusion. Transform the old into the new.

Wednesday 25th

You may find yourself looking back at the past and towards the future. This is a pivotal point and you can sit still and look at both sides. What skills have you brought into the present and are still using? What new skills would you like to learn?

Thursday 26th

The Moon moves into your travel sector today, but it is making uneasy connections to practically every planet. You may feel pushed, pulled, ignored, overstimulated or totally drained. Your emotions could erupt like a volcano, so try to keep a low profile and nurture yourself.

Friday 27th

You are irritated beyond words. Restlessness is a big problem and you cannot focus on any one thing. You will need to do grounding activities such as walking in nature, physical exercise or getting in touch with your body by feeding it healthy food. Find your inner calm now.

Saturday 28th

There is a vibrant energy now between Venus and Jupiter, which can help you come back down to Earth. Venus wants intimacy, so Jupiter grants it with his lucky charms. Venus wants delicious food, so Jupiter serves it on a platter. Venus wants a little luxury, so Jupiter happily delivers it. Use this energy well.

Sunday 29th

You may find yourself doing some Sunday business hours today. Researching or getting a project ready will occupy you, and you will gain satisfaction from time well spent. Talking, either on the phone or through text messages, may also fill up your day, but it will all benefit your career.

Monday 3oth

Mars is at the last degree of your creative sector. You
must now look at unfinished projects or those you put
to one side and meant to return to. You have a burst of
energy and motivation to get these sorted now before
your attention shifts to another area.

Tuesday 31st

Mars is now marching on to your health and duties
sector to sit beside Saturn. Saturn holds him long
enough to give him the itinerary for the next few weeks.
Step up your fitness regime and put everything you have
got into it. Have your health checked now too.

APRIL
....

Wednesday 1st
You can start to build upon your dreams now, and
your emotional needs can be expressed easily. Your
connection to a divine source, if you believe in one, can
be heightened at this time. This can also be a time when
you take a relationship to a deeper level.

Thursday 2nd
Self-indulgence might just be the flavour of the day.
The Moon enters your dreams sector, which means that
you may be lazy or want to be alone. You may get fired
up with thoughts of a spiritual retreat or a vision quest.
Enjoy the silence today.

Friday 3rd
Venus enters your career sector and, as she rules money,
this is indeed a good time. She will help you to assess
where you are being valued, or not, in the workplace.
Self-worth may come into question, and you should
review this in regards to career and prospects.

Saturday 4th

This is a good day for love and romance, where you will continue to take connections to deeper levels. You can talk together about shared dreams and goals. Be careful to stay on the side of reality, however, as illusions and pipe dreams may steer you away into unknown waters.

Sunday 5th

The Moon enters your sign, which may make you more self-centred. You may be checking schedules and making sure that all is in order. Take control over big projects and make sure you are on top of them. Self-expression could be blown out of all proportion today if you self-promote.

Monday 6th

You have a chance to transform something in a very big way. This could be something about you and your identity. It could be as simple as a haircut or as big as an attitude shift. There could also be issues with the law or other types of power struggles today.

Tuesday 7th

Mars and Uranus are locked in a conflict today, so there could be trouble ahead in your daily routines and travel sectors. These two planets can be quite volatile, so it is likely to be an aggressive time. Elsewhere, your money sector is activated by the Moon. Hold on to whatever funds you have.

Wednesday 8th

Today's Full Moon in your money and possessions sector will highlight any issues you have around what is valuable to you. What success have you gained in this area over the last six months? What are you able to let go of now? Aim for harmony and beauty.

Thursday 9th

You may have an enquiring mind and want to explore areas that are forbidden. Your sense of humour could be on the darker side now. The Moon is making difficult connections to Mars and Uranus, so be aware that tensions may erupt.

Friday 10th

Recent tensions ease a little and you find yourself back in control of your mind and bubbling temper. There is something emotional nagging at you that needs to be aired, but you will need to bide your time on this. Paternal figures may feature today, and will have something to teach you.

Saturday 11th

Family matters are foremost now. Home and hearth need attention. A family outing or educating children could be just the thing. Lead by example and show younger generations that however far they stray, home is with the people who love and support them. Encourage growth.

Sunday 12th

For the next couple of weeks, you will be talking and learning about a topic that is completely new to you. This may capture your imagination and motivate you to explore at a great depth. This is due to Mercury entering your sex, death and rebirth sector, encouraging you to research the mysteries of life.

Monday 13th

You will return to projects that come from the heart today. There is something you have started that you are now emotionally attached to. You want to see this as an outward expression of who you are. Create, express and show it off. Claim your moment of glory.

Tuesday 14th

Power issues surface once more. You must either take control of a situation or be controlled by it. You can see clearly where you have been giving your power away and will no longer stand for it. Your ego may take a hit in the process, but this is no bad thing. Learn from it.

Wednesday 15th

Today brings more tension between the two sectors that deal with sex, death and rebirth and your daily routine and health. The Sun is highlighting where these areas may be draining you. Finances that are tied up with someone else are also in the spotlight now.

Thursday 16th

Making or getting a health check-up will benefit you today. You need to look after yourself as there are areas in your daily routine that are draining you. Venus and the Moon lend you the motivation to do something just for you today. Looking after number one is important now.

Friday 17th

Being with a special person and enjoying quality time is all you require today. A romantic night in with your loved one will put you on cloud nine. If alone, thoughts will arise about how you can relate to those deep parts of yourself.

Saturday 18th

Mercury and Venus are talking together today. They are discussing how you can combine your career with your need for deep exploration of the secret and forbidden. You may feel like a detective, and could unearth intrigue in your workplace. Don't take it too seriously. Just have fun with it.

Sunday 19th

Do you remember those seeds you planted at the equinox? Those intentions and affirmations can start germinating now that the Sun has shifted into an Earth sign. Things will begin to develop in your travel area, so you may start thinking about holidays. Where would you like to explore?

Monday 20th

You may find yourself feeling highly motivated today with positive energy and plans for the summer ahead. There is a strong sense of something turning around for you. Look ahead and form some great ideas and plans. These could involve another person and you could be travelling together.

Tuesday 21st

This is a romantic day where the Moon is making a connection to Mars and Venus. They are being held at an equal distance emotionally, and this is taking place in your career and daily routine sectors. Is there someone at work that you find attractive?

Wednesday 22nd

The Moon is on its way into your travel sector now. You will be thinking about higher education and exploring new lands. Foreign cultures may appeal to you and tug on your heartstrings. You could be yearning for new experiences at this time. Tie this into your travel plans.

Thursday 23rd

A New Moon occurs in your travel sector. This Moon is ruled by Venus, who loves money, beauty and harmony. You might find yourself spending on some luxury item or holiday. Do not feel guilty. This will be a good investment if done for the right reasons.

Friday 24th

Enjoy a day of easy, upbeat energy. If you can go with the flow, you will discover harmony in all areas. You will be able to complete all of your tasks on time and to a satisfactory standard. Well done. You excel in this type of energy.

Saturday 25th

You would most like to spend today planning your holiday, but chores will probably take up most of your time instead. You cannot express yourself easily now. This is a passing phase so don't fret too much. Your boss may have something to say that should be listened to.

Sunday 26th

Pluto, the planet of power, control and transformation, goes retrograde now. He does this in your creative expression sector, and is asking you to think about how you radiate who you are. Other planets in difficult connections can make today interesting, radical or even revolutionary.

Monday 27th

Friendship groups will give you the support needed today. Network and research your travel plans. Educate yourself by the experiences of friends who can give good advice. You will feel part of the tribe and comforted by being in the company of others. Friends are family.

Tuesday 28th

Emotions are pulled towards an unknown future now. This may feel like the last chance to do something you have been yearning to do. This will involve your family, mother or close friends. Let yourself be open to suggestions, and do what you have to do.

Wednesday 29th

Feeling restricted or not in control will burden you today. This is owing to the Moon being opposite retrograde Pluto. You may want to hide away because you do not have the strength to deal with it right now. Sit and listen to the advice of your elders.

Thursday 30th

This is a day to be under the duvet with ice cream and a good book. You will likely have very little motivation and feel rather overwhelmed. Lie low and sort your colouring pencils or arrange your books in alphabetical order. You want a distraction from problems. Do it the Virgo way, by organising your life!

MAY

....

Friday 1st

You may need to put your hand over your mouth today.
Mercury, who is well known for speaking his mind, is
right on top of Uranus, who likes to shock and surprise.
As well as that, the Moon is opposite Mars, who can be
violent and aggressive. This is a volatile day.

Saturday 2nd

The Moon moves into Virgo today, so you can self-
indulge or put your best foot forward and show what
you are made of. Tidying the home or checking your
schedule for the next week will bring satisfaction.
However, don't be a martyr. Use this time for you.

Sunday 3rd

You are likely to have more of a handle on what needs
to be done now. Take control of all the little chores that
have been piling up. Conversation becomes easier. You
can settle your restless mind knowing that all is in order.

Monday 4th

Taking care of your money and environment are the main issues of the day. Try to bring balance and harmony into these areas. Mercury has nothing to say, so you may feel foggy. Rest assured that this feeling will pass very quickly.

Tuesday 5th

There is a general shift in the universe now. Look outwards, and make important and lasting connections. For you, this will involve your career, fathers and bosses, patriarchy and leadership. This is an eighteen-month shift, so take note of what happens along the way.

Wednesday 6th

Trivial conversations may bore you now, and you are likely to prefer intrigue and fascinating mysteries. It is hard to make small talk and you may disconnect from shallow people. Reach out to those who can talk on the same level as you.

Thursday 7th

A Full Moon in your communication sector brings an intensity that will excite you. There is so much more out there waiting to be discovered. You may have already had a glimpse of this. What were you doing six months ago that led you down a rabbit hole?

Friday 8th

Look back to the past and review the skills you have
learnt and brought with you into the present. Higher
education and explorations come back into mind now,
and you may be thinking about past failures. Do you
want a second chance?

Saturday 9th

Today, you will need to feel more grounded. You may
feel flighty and restless, but the chances are that you will
know exactly what to do. Physical exercise, food or walks
in nature will take up most of your weekend. This is time
well spent, so enjoy it.

Sunday 10th

Mercury races through the last part of your travel sector
today. What have you learnt regarding foreign lands or
higher education recently? You may have made some
rushed decisions here. Go back and review these themes
now. There may be something you have overlooked.

Monday 11th

Saturn goes retrograde now, and there will be lessons
to learn in your creative expression sector. This is likely
to be more about how you present yourself. Behaviours
and habits will come under close scrutiny now. Will the
real Virgo please stand up?

Tuesday 12th

Mercury, the master researcher and communicator, now moves into your career sector. This can make you more efficient in the workplace. Make the most of this time to network and investigate how you can advance your career. Mercury may also inject a little laughter in the office.

Wednesday 13th

Venus begins her retrograde period today, and she starts by traversing your career sector. You may find colleagues, or yourself, leaving the workplace and moving on. You may be torn between committing and breaking off work engagements. Vacillating and procrastinating will become themes at work.

Thursday 14th

Mars has shifted into your relationship sector. Your energy levels will be boosted, and you will be able to connect deeply with your partner or love interest. Mars energy can be aggressive and direct, but today it is more like walking on water or clouds.

Friday 15th

Jupiter, the lawgiver and expander, goes retrograde today, and begins retracing his steps in your creative sector. You will be asked not to go too far when expressing your needs. You will feel restricted in your freedom, but this will be for a good reason. This will make sense when Jupiter is direct again.

Saturday 16th

The Moon, in your romance sector, is not playing fairly with Venus today. You may become selfish and needy. You may disregard your partner's needs in favour of your own, causing tension or bad feeling. Keeping a low profile can avoid these issues getting out of hand.

Sunday 17th

You may feel an urge to get up and go today. You want to start something, maybe even an argument. Shared finances, control and sex are all potential issues. Tension from yesterday could get deeper and more intimate or personal. This will illuminate who is really in control. Be considerate and direct.

Monday 18th

This is a good day for making yourself heard at work. You may have a burning desire to meet with your boss to suggest a change or even ask for a bonus. Ideas will be well received and you will feel proud about being courageous enough to approach management. Well done.

Tuesday 19th

After yesterday's boost of confidence, you may now feel less sure about voicing your opinions at work. However, this is not your fault. Venus retrograde is actually responsible. She is connecting to the Moon, hitting you in an emotional space. This feeling will pass.

Wednesday 20th

The Sun moves into your career sector today. There is already a lot of activity here, but the Sun will illuminate any dark corners and put both Mercury and Venus in their places. If you are in the shadows now, you can come out and show your own light.

Thursday 21st

This is quite a week at work for you, and today you will be asked for your opinions and ideas. You are being listened to. Your skills with research, methodology, bookkeeping and databases are being recognised now. If you are a shrinking violet then prepare to come into full bloom.

Friday 22nd

A New Moon occurs in your career sector today, and this may herald the start of something new and valuable in your work life. Use this time to set intentions and affirmations regarding career and advancing it – if that is what you want.

Saturday 23rd

There may be some agitation today, as the Moon confronts Mars in your relationship sector. You could feel a little drained and just not in the mood for love. However, you could also want your own way and may have a tantrum if you don't get it.

Sunday 24th

Your friends understand, don't they? You have had enough of work and relationships this week, so will now turn towards friends. Out of everyone, you can confide in them the most, and you truly feel a sense of belonging with these people. Friendships can offer nourishment now.

Monday 25th

A lot of fun could be had by networking on social media today. Charity or goodwill causes will appeal to you, and you may find yourself signing up to support many of them. This will make you feel wholesome and satisfied, and you should be proud for helping others.

Tuesday 26th

You may feel down today, but will not be able to put your finger on where this is coming from. It is just a vague feeling of unrest. This is because the Moon is opposite Pluto, who likes to control or transform something. Use this energy to change that frown into a smile.

Wednesday 27th

It is time to retreat and be alone. You are not in the mood to socialise or engage in work activities now. Do something that satisfies you alone. Try to keep a fire burning inside, but it does not need to be a roaring flame. You can be lazy now.

Thursday 28th

Mercury leaves your work sector and moves into your friendship groups today. This is another great time. Networking, socialising and joining new groups will be a theme over the next couple of weeks. There may be a lot of fun and laughter. Raised spirits will be infectious.

Friday 29th

The Moon in Virgo is asking you to be your typical self and get out the planners, timetables and schedules. Making something neat and tidy usually fills your heart with peace. Also, take this time to check on your health and make sure you have not missed anything.

Saturday 30th

How do you serve others? You may be a sounding board or a shoulder to cry on today, as you have the knack of directing lost souls in the right direction. Who will guide you in return? Use this time to assess where your energy flows, and if any comes back to you.

Sunday 31st

It's time to balance the books and organise the home.
Harmony and beauty around your personal space are so
important for you to enjoy being there. Moving furniture
into a different place can brighten your environment.
Play with this now and see if it feels different.

JUNE

....

Monday 1st

June begins with the Moon still in your money and possessions sector. You will be reviewing what money is going in and what money is going out. Thinking about what you do not have is futile. You need to accumulate in order to speculate. Weigh up the pros and cons.

Tuesday 2nd

Conversations might be intriguing now. They may also be deep and intense. Venus and Mars are clashing, which could lead to a battle of the sexes. There is likely to be some backtracking on commitments and decisions made with partners now, both in love and in work.

Wednesday 3rd

Women will win the day. Venus is right in the heat of the Sun, so you may see female influences becoming powerful at work. Women's voices, and especially their protestations, will be important now. There could be an uprising of sorts in the workplace.

Thursday 4th

Watch out for needless aggravation in relationships today. Someone could be exposed as a bully. Will it be you? Take refuge in close family or in education. Keeping your attention fixed outside of personal relationships may help to avoid trouble.

Friday 5th

Today's Full Moon in your family sector brings a restless urge to get out and explore. You are not satisfied with the limits and boundaries set by the family environment and want to break free. Have you already escaped the confines of your family?

Saturday 6th

You should try to express yourself today. You may wonder what your purpose is and how you can shine your unique light in the world. Just be yourself. People love your sense of order amid chaos. Children and laughter may offer the boost you need.

Sunday 7th

When you are on top form, you can be a vessel for others to let off steam or rant. Review who is there when you need to do the same. You are calm in another person's crisis but often fall to pieces in your own.

Monday 8th

The Moon now hits the retrograde planets in your
creativity sector. Find a way of taking back your own
personal power without causing unrest. You may feel
unlucky at the moment, but this will be short-lived.
The law may feature in today's proceedings. Karma may
also come calling.

Tuesday 9th

You have your own limits, and may see today just how
far people will go to overstep them. Daily routines
comfort you, but you will recognise that there are only
so many hours in the day to get things done. Overdoing
it will not help your energy levels.

Wednesday 10th

Today could go two very different ways. You may be
stuck in a fiction and unable to see the reality. You may
feel foggy or surreal about a loved one. Alternatively,
you may now see the fog lifting as rose-tinted glasses
finally come off.

Thursday 11th

Time spent with a loved one can be romantic again now. There is a long and winding road to walk down with that special someone. You may think that you will never reach the end of it, so make sure that you enjoy the journey.

Friday 12th

Indecision may stop you today. The Moon is confronting Venus in her retrograde, making you have an on/off feeling about your relationships. Do not make any commitments until you are absolutely sure of what the options are. Take a break to process this if needed.

Saturday 13th

This is a difficult day, given the current Venus retrograde. The Moon is now sitting with both Mars, who rules energy, and Neptune, who dissolves things. This could very well be a make or break day within relationships. You could react with anger or switch off completely.

Sunday 14th

The Moon shifts gears into your sex, death and rebirth sector today. Whatever the outcome of yesterday, you can now explore the whys and wherefores of what happened. It is an intense time of discovery and excavation of your own soul. This is the best thing to do right now.

Monday 15th

Heart and mind battles may occur today. You may struggle to think clearly, with emotions jumping all over the place. Mercury will go retrograde again this week, so use the next few days to back up devices and check all travel plans and contracts. Take your mind off your troubles.

Tuesday 16th

Are you feeling stuck? You will probably need a push and a shove to get going today. Your emotions tell you to stay where you are, but you will find a helpful motion if you put one foot in front of the other. Get something started.

Wednesday 17th

It may feel as though you have gone back to school to learn everything from the beginning again. You cannot get a grip on daily routines and you may actually become unwell. It is as if you have handed in a bad piece of homework, but have no energy left to do it all again.

Thursday 18th

Mercury retrograde begins in your area of friendships and social groups. As Mercury is known for speaking his mind, this is not a great area for you to have him in. Remember at all times to ask yourself this before you speak; is it true, is it kind, is it useful? Sometimes if you can't say anything nice, it's best not to say anything at all

Friday 19th

Today will have a Scorpian flavour, which means it
could be intense and secretive. There could be power
struggles, as well as both endings and beginnings. You
may get a glimpse into long-term plans at work. These
could be your own personal goals. What did you have in
mind? What are you aiming for?

Saturday 20th

Mars and Jupiter are having tactic talks now, and Mars
in your relationship sector is getting a big boost from
Jupiter in your creative sector. Your drive and energy
are about to get bigger. Take care not to utilise Mars'
habit of being aggressive. Avoid bullying a loved one.
Play nice today, Virgo.

Sunday 21st

A New Moon and solar eclipse fall in your friends
sector today. The longest day has a shadow over it. Look
around your friendship groups both physically and
online. Who is lurking in the shadows? Who wants to be
seen and heard more? Is it perhaps you?

Monday 22nd

You often trust your friends more than your family,
and you feel safe in their company as they nurture and
nourish your growth. If you can become vulnerable
with them, the connection will deepen. Showing open
wounds to friends can help trigger the healing process.

Tuesday 23rd

Today is definitely one where you must go through the daily grind then hibernate under a blanket. Yet another planet goes retrograde, and this time it is Neptune. He is responsible for illusion, delusion, retreats and isolation. He is in your relationship sector, so maybe you can hide with a loved one. Time to build yourself a blanket fort and camp out until the weather changes.

Wednesday 24th

When a big planet like Neptune shifts, it is felt collectively. This triggers a change of direction within the current theme. You and a loved one may feel like drifting off to sea in a pea-green boat. Does being washed up on an unknown island appeal to you?

Thursday 25th

Some pressure is lifted today in your career sector. Decisions become easier and you will no longer be wavering about commitments. Someone or something has left the playing field and has now made the path clear for you. It is time to step up your game.

Friday 26th

You may feel caught in the crossfire in your relationships. This can also feel like a tug of war with you tied in the middle. Your energy and drive are being pulled in different directions. Learn from past mistakes. There is no going back. Look to the future and march on.

Saturday 27th

You have reached a crucial point in your relationships.
Is there any unfinished business still to deal with? You
cannot move on until issues have been resolved fully.
This needs your attention now, so tackle it right away
and deal with it fully. Otherwise, it will come back to
haunt you later.

Sunday 28th

There will be a sense of relief today as Mars enters
your sex, death and rebirth sector. He is now in his
domain and is much happier. He can help start new
ventures with vigour and passion. You can put all
of your energy into deep and intense activities now,
don't be afraid to start something involving now, if
you have the time for it.

Monday 29th

There is an unpleasant connection between the Moon
and your creative sector today, but this will soon pass.
In the meantime, try to ignore it and concentrate on
projects initiated by Mars. You need to stay motivated
and passionate. Keep focusing on your new project,
use this to spur yourself onwards.

Tuesday 3oth

The Moon gives an added intensity to any Martian pursuits today. Conversations can be deep and meaningful. There may be some huge power struggles around self-expression, so stand your ground and speak your truth. Refuse to be silenced, unless you know you are in the wrong. If you are right, make sure your voice is heard – stand by your convictions.

JULY

....

Wednesday 1st

Conversations with friends and social groups may
be difficult. Mercury is in the heat of the Sun, which
means that you cannot communicate very well. This
may lead to misunderstandings. It may also produce
some ingenious thinking, if you can just focus on one
thing at a time.

Thursday 2nd

Saturn returns to a critical point in your creative sector
today. This could be about unfinished business. It
could also be about love, and how you create soulful
connections. The Moon, in your family sector, may
bring some agitation or deep emotions to the surface.
You may feel trapped.

Friday 3rd

Running away from family problems is not the answer.
Educating yourself on why these problems persist, is.
You may be the wanderer in the family and want to
explore the world through travel or education. Bring
back your wisdom and share it with your kin.

Saturday 4th

Emotional needs are filled by your creativity and self-expression now. Say what you feel without fear of being judged. This is a brave and courageous thing to do. Showing your true essence is the raw, creative expression of your soul truths.

Sunday 5th

A Full Moon in your creative sector will highlight your efforts so far in a project. Have you been putting everything you have got into it? There is also a lunar eclipse, which suggests you may have abandoned the project entirely. Use this time to see what you have in front of you.

Monday 6th

There is some lovely energy now between your duties and career sectors. Venus and the Moon are working together to make these areas run smoothly. This is also the time to review your health and diet. You may want delicious foods, but are they ultimately good for you?

Tuesday 7th

Are you taking on too many duties? Venus in your career sector asks that you find a balance between work and everything else that you must do to get through the day. If you have been exhausting yourself recently then now is the time to think about what to let go.

Wednesday 8th

Spend time on important relationships today. There could be some tension between friends and lovers. You may be unsure who to spend time with. The Moon in your relationship sector suggests that the best plan is to be with someone special. Avoid power struggles and crossed words.

Thursday 9th

You may feel guilty about neglecting something at work today. It is not clear what it is, but you have a niggling feeling that will not go away. You may have let someone down because you wanted something for yourself. Try to put the situation right.

Friday 10th

You should attend to those little jobs in the workplace today. You are the best at knowing where everything is, and people rely on your organisational skills. Perhaps some time off has made you realise this. Being methodical is one of your greatest gifts, but it can leave others feeling helpless.

Saturday 11th

As the Moon shifts, your emotional needs turn towards darker subjects. You may feel an urge to start something new, but you seem to have forgotten about the things that have not been completed. Exploring life's deeper mysteries appeals more than finishing up old courses of study. Check to make sure you are not neglecting something important.

Sunday 12th

Mercury has finished his retrograde period through your social sector, which means you must now think about what was under review. When he retraces his steps, you will confront the same issues again and approach them differently. This will involve friends and wider social activities, including social media groups.

Monday 13th

Some fog may clear with Mercury direct again. Take another look at any problems that may have seemed insurmountable recently. You may now be able to see a way through. Put one foot in front of the other and make progress. Take it slowly and look at every possible angle.

Tuesday 14th

You may find an innovative solution to a problem today, as bright ideas and light-bulb moments may come along. The Sun and Jupiter are making a great connection, which encourages you to expand on theories. Luck will be on your side. Go with the flow of this excellent energy.

Wednesday 15th

Power and control are the issues for today, and these will manifest in your creative expression sector. You may hear a voice that cleverly manipulates and seduces others. Yours may even be that voice. Another theme will be that of change, and it will be glaringly obvious now.

Thursday 16th

The Moon enters your career sector, which may make you feel unsure about your value and role at work. Insecurities about the job you do may bubble up to the surface. This Moon phase will pass quickly, and you would do best to sit with these feelings and review them another time.

Friday 17th

The Moon meets Venus, who soothes your insecurities. She will bring harmony and balance to your work life, and may give you the added confidence you have been missing lately. This can be an empowering energy, and it should be tapped into. You are plenty capable. Stand tall.

Saturday 18th

Your mood will turn towards friends, particularly your close tribe. These are the ones to go to when you need sound advice, encouragement and support. You should be held and comforted by dear friends today. Remove the armour and prepare to open up.

Sunday 19th

You should express your deepest feelings now. The Moon is meeting Mercury, who likes to talk and share stories, so this is the perfect chance for a campfire with friends or for a meeting with spiritual people. Sharing and caring are the words for today. Raise the group vibration and share the love.

Monday 20th

A New Moon occurs in your social sector today. As with all New Moons, this is the universe asking what you want. What would you like to achieve now with friends and activity groups? Start something or just make intentions and affirmations regarding friends and family.

Tuesday 21st

There is a restless feeling in the air because the Moon has moved into your dreams and retreat area. You want to burn like a glorious flame, but are feeling burnt out. You might be indecisive and err on the lazy side. Retreat into your own little world. It will not hurt.

Wednesday 22nd

The Sun moves into your dreams sector today, helping to warm up your solitary retreat. This will burn away any illusions you may have been having, and help you to see the way forwards. Time alone would be healthy. Be sure to use it productively.

Thursday 23rd

You are in your element when given paperwork to file or a bookshelf to categorise. Getting on with something systematic will bring that sense of satisfaction today. You will get an adrenaline rush through restoring order and harmony. This is a day well spent.

Friday 24th

You may not be able to think straight today, and feelings about your relationships may preoccupy you. If you look deeper into these feelings, you may find that the real problem lies with you and not the other person. The Moon opposite your shadow area will bring this up for investigation.

Saturday 25th

Introducing beauty and harmony into the home environment will bring you pleasure today. Try tweaking your style a little or rearranging the furniture. Thinking about how and where you spend money will also be on your mind. There is no guilt required, just a little reckoning.

Sunday 26th

Today, you are looking at how you divide your time between friends. You may be spending more time with friends on social media than in person. Sometimes, online friends can see a side that you do not show to your oldest friends. Why is that?

Monday 27th

A tense energy surrounds many areas of life today. You will prefer meaningful conversations, but there are disagreements to be had. The workplace and relationships are hard to juggle now. You cannot bat for all sides, so sit this one out and keep your head down.

Tuesday 28th

Recent tensions will ease, as Jupiter makes a friendly connection to Neptune in your relationships sector. Take time with a special person and discuss shared dreams and vision quests. Jupiter will add some good luck and humour to the pleasant atmosphere you build with a loved one today.

Wednesday 29th

This is an ideal day to connect with your family and inject a good mood into the home. Stories about exciting adventures from the past can bring laughter, as well as a revived passion to book an exotic holiday. You may even begin to plan a trip.

Thursday 30th

Many discussions will be taking place today, and big plans may start to take root. This may also be a time where gossip amongst friends could get out of control and arguments arise. Conversely, there could be lots of light-hearted banter with friends.

Friday 31st

You may want to return to creative projects or even an old rhetoric now. The huge planets in this sector are making it difficult for you, as they are all in retrograde. This may feel as if you have writer's block. Do not worry, however. You have not lost your passion.

AUGUST

....

Saturday 1st

Power and control issues may occur within your friendship groups or on social media today. Mercury, in your social sector, is directly opposite Pluto, the lord of power. This may make you very sensitive to criticism, and likely to respond defensively. This could be a volatile day, so try to stay out of arguments.

Sunday 2nd

The Sun and Uranus are meeting today, which means something is heating up that could possibly erupt. This will disturb your peaceful dream space, and may also have an impact on your travel sector. This could be a revolution, but it could also be something unique and innovative.

Monday 3rd

A Full Moon in your health and duties sector can illuminate the places where you need to radically change routines. You may have already done this and are now seeing some success. Brave new ideas can change the way you manage your everyday routines.

Tuesday 4th

Please watch out for accidents today. Mars, the warrior, is in his own sign of Aries, and in the area he rules. For you, he is in your sex, death and rebirth sector. He is also confronting Jupiter, who likes to extend and expand. Whatever happens will be on a large scale.

Wednesday 5th

Hold your loved ones close to you today. This is a sweet day where you can share your deepest feelings and wishes. You can have dreamy conversations and plan some time away together. Look for a spiritual connection now. Seek the divine.

Thursday 6th

Venus reaches the point of the north node today. This point is like looking into the future and hearing the voice that beckons. You should make plans about money, possessions, love, beauty and harmony whilst Venus is in this position. Think quickly and manifest that future.

Friday 7th

Your friends and social sector will now get an infusion from Venus. As she rules harmony, you will find that any ongoing disputes or feuds will be forgotten. You may find yourself acting as a mediator or being the person who brings two different groups together.

Saturday 8th

This is a great day for staying home with your partner
or best friend. Shut the doors so the two of you can
put the world to rights. You may also be connecting
with a divine source, possibly by praying, meditating or
exploring different religions.

Sunday 9th

Today, there is a nagging feeling of being restricted. You
may find your freedom of speech is curbed, leaving you
feeling worthless. Any artistic projects are slowing down
now, but this is all because of the Moon. Remember that
this is a passing phase. Stick with it.

Monday 10th

It may feel as though you are walking in volcanic lava
today. Keep a low profile and concentrate on the job
in hand. The goalposts could shift at any time and you
need to stay focused, or you may slip into the volcano.

Tuesday 11th

Mercury is racing through your dreams sector today, and
makes an uneasy aspect to the Moon. Discussions may
now become personal and raise some deep emotions.
You may have found your connection to something
spiritual, but lost it again. Sit and listen.

Wednesday 12th

A sociable, waning Moon wanders through your career sector today. You are being asked to let go of something related to work. You are in two minds about this. Pay attention to the minor details first. Do they serve you or are you serving them?

Thursday 13th

This is another day where you will see power struggles. Mars and Pluto are at odds in your sex, death and rebirth, and creative sectors. Mars in Aries wants to forge ahead, but Pluto wants an ending. Consider what needs to be removed or transformed in these areas.

Friday 14th

There may be some manipulation and exploitation around now. You may feel underestimated or undervalued. Old structures are being torn down or are crumbling around you. This is making room for something better to move in. This is an intense time of change.

Saturday 15th

A very supportive meeting between the Moon and Venus happens today in your social sector, and you will feel nurtured and empowered by friendship groups. Relying on their support will make the recent difficult times a little easier. You may have a boost of energy and dreams may seem like possibilities now.

Sunday 16th

Uranus, the disruptor, goes retrograde now in your travel sector. Plans and itineraries could fall apart, vehicles may suddenly become unreliable and good ideas may now look like bad ones. You might be faced with brick walls, but you will be able to topple them by using Uranus' energy to think things through.

Monday 17th

You may feel tired, drained of energy and inclined to be alone to lick your wounds today. You are irritated and grouchy, so make some time for yourself with a good book or film. You are not in the mood to deal with other people.

Tuesday 18th

There is a New Moon today in your dream sector. You may experience this as an urge to simply retreat. Deep inside, there is a need to be authentic and genuine. However, be sure to do some inner work before showing your full glory to the world.

Wednesday 19th

The Moon is now in Virgo, and you can begin to process the thoughts activated yesterday. Formulate plans to manifest your goals. You do not want to be a shrinking violet any more. Looking after number one is the first step to seeing these goals come to fruition.

Thursday 20th

Mercury enters Virgo today, and is likely to fill your head with ideas. He is your planetary ruler, so you feel more like yourself now. You are able to listen to that inner voice and use discernment. Mercury will teach you how to dedicate yourself to a task and receive a reward later. Do the research now.

Friday 21st

The Moon moves into your money and possessions sector today. A need to feel safe and secure in your environment may make you moody. You may worry about finances and overspending, but have an urge to spend at the same time. Find that happy balance between necessity and luxury.

Saturday 22nd

The Sun enters Virgo today, marking the beginning of your birthday month. This will help you to feel revitalised, and there will be a renewed sense of purpose and who you are. This is a great energy if you have been hiding under a bushel. Come on out and shine.

Sunday 23rd

Deep, intense conversations attract you now. Small talk will just not do. You are researching subjects that are mysterious and esoteric. There may be trips or visits to people and places that interest you on a deeper level. However, mundane chores may take you away from wider interests.

Monday 24th

Mars and Saturn are not very friendly today. There is a tension between your creative activities and your love interests. Saturn is trying to teach you about boundaries, while Mars wants to march straight through them. Keep your boundaries safe and do not breach those of others. Be respectful.

Tuesday 25th

Spending time with family should be fun and adventurous today, but there could be some issues with maternal and paternal roles clashing. Who is the boss? Who makes the decisions? Elsewhere, there may be some nice surprises and good news to come. Mercury will connect to Uranus, so expect the unexpected.

Wednesday 26th

There is a great deal of loving energy today. Your social circle may get much bigger now. Do you have enough love to go around? You may feel that you do not have time to please everyone. Friends will understand if you need a break. Do not overstretch yourself.

Thursday 27th

Venus adds some light-hearted energy to your friendships today. Allow yourself to drift into a fantasy scenario, but remember that it is not real. You may also be making small sacrifices for other people. Energy and drive are boosted by considering past adventures.

Friday 28th

There is still a surreal atmosphere floating around. You may be planning a trip that is unlikely to happen, but will have fun thinking about it anyway. Contemplate unusual holidays abroad. This could even be the idea of making a permanent move. Putting down roots in a foreign land appeals now.

Saturday 29th

The Moon is making a lot of unexpected connections today. This will affect your emotions, and may be very draining. Your creative, social, personal and relationship sectors are all involved. This may be a good day to spend alone. Hide away with a book or a new planner.

Sunday 30th

You should check in with your health today if you still feel emotionally drained after yesterday. There may be clashes within friendship groups concerning control issues. Mercury will add to the confusion, and there may well be gossip that you will need to ignore. Do not be the gossiper.

Monday 31st

Your passion gets an extra boost today. Mars is in your sex, death and rebirth sector, and can help you explore these areas. Reconnect with a person or a project with which you have shared finances and investments. This is also a good day to sort out taxes.

SEPTEMBER

. . . .

Tuesday 1st

The Moon moves into your relationship sector today,
heralding a time of deep connection with loved ones
and friends. You may be empathic, but you may also
be misguided. Others may try to pull the wool over
your eyes and absorb your energy. Remember your
personal boundaries.

Wednesday 2nd

Venus moves into your social sector today. She is sat
opposite Saturn, the teacher. Together, they will be able to
discuss where things are out of balance. You may be letting
the wrong people into your life and shutting the right ones
out. Review the connections you have with friends.

Thursday 3rd

Today, it is Mercury's turn for a lesson from Saturn. This
one is about your self-expression. Mercury can be known
for speaking his mind, but he can also go over the top
with it. Saturn is asking that you consider whether you
are showing off or faithfully showing your true colours.

Friday 4th

There may be a battle of the sexes today. Females are
likely to win this, as Mercury is giving Venus the power
of speech. Mars is being forthright and belligerent
in your sex sector. He is pushy and relentless. Think
carefully before you speak and remember to show
compassion. This will lead to victory.

Saturday 5th

Mercury shifts into your money sector today. He is
the planet associated with merchants, so now is a
great chance to buy and sell. He can be like a good
car salesman and make a profit with his selling skills.
Investing or selling something now is favourable.

Sunday 6th

Venus shifts signs today, and dances into your dreams
sector. This will bring beauty and harmony to any time
spent alone. She will give you the courage and strength
to pursue whatever you perceive to be out of reach. She
may also bring the money needed to follow your dreams.

Monday 7th

The Moon in your travel sector once again meets
Uranus. This coupling may make you restless and want
to run away to foreign lands. This feeling is made bigger
by the Moon's connection to Jupiter. If you are unable to
run, satisfy yourself by researching places of interest.

Tuesday 8th

Your career is activated by the Moon now. The
theme here is that something needs to change or be
transformed for the better. These are positive changes.
What have you dreamt about, but not had the courage to
reach for? Try now, while the energy is good.

Wednesday 9th

Today's Virgo Sun will bring good luck your way. This
may be connected to your creative endeavours or sole
purpose. There may be a breakthrough now, and you
could find an open door or a path that is meant to be
followed. Spiritual connections are within reach.

Thursday 10th

Mars goes retrograde in your sex, death and rebirth sector.
This will no doubt be a frustrating time where you will
be unable to get what you want in the usual ways. Review
where you may be too aggressive and careless when
pursuing something. Be careful with travel now.

Friday 11th

The weekend is almost here, and the Moon is in your
social sector. This is good news if you have any catching
up with friends or family to do. Fantasies and illusions
can be seen for what they really are now. You could feel
disappointed in some friends. Falsity falls away.

Saturday 12th

Try thrashing around some ideas within your friendship
groups. Try something new or just approach a topic from
a different angle. You will not be upsetting people by
being radical, instead, they will likely follow your lead.
Think outside the box now and surprise yourself.

Sunday 13th

Your emotions and actions may not be working together
now. This is the Moon activating the Mars retrograde in
your sex, death and rebirth sector. Don't force anything
because it will backfire on you. Wait until this phase
passes. Jupiter is now direct and brings more joy into
your creative sector.

Monday 14th

This is a lovely day to be courageous and do something
you have not dared to before. This could be something
as simple as going to the cinema alone, having a date
with yourself or connecting with a spiritual group.
Change is on the way, and it will come from within.

Tuesday 15th

Today, you may be thinking about skills learnt in the past and how to use them again to benefit you now. There will be a little shock to your system as you do something that frightens you. It may even be something that makes you retreat into solitude.

Wednesday 16th

Today's Moon in Virgo wants you to spend the day quietly and alone. If at work, just concentrate on the job in hand. If at home, simply rest and recharge your batteries. Don't think about taking on any tasks, as you are unlikely to complete them.

Thursday 17th

Today's New Moon in Virgo will pose two questions: how much you do for other people? And, how much do you do for yourself? You may consider starting a new health and fitness regime or making small changes to daily routines. Make mini resolutions at this time.

Friday 18th

Look at where you are overstretched and let unnecessary duties go. You may have taken on more than you can manage with creative projects. Have you been a bit narcissistic lately? Do you feel bad about it? Small children and their games may feature today.

Saturday 19th

There is a difficult energy around today. You may feel
stuck in a situation and want to run away. The trouble
is, your feet may seem to be glued to the spot. This
is an opportunity to delve deeper into the situation
before making any hasty moves. Look for the golden
egg in this heavy atmosphere.

Sunday 20th

Today, you may be prone to outbursts. You may say what
is in your heart, but other people will not want to hear
it and you could be made to feel selfish. Look out for
arguments involving travel plans or spirituality. Try to
contain any anger you feel. This will soon pass.

Monday 21st

Family will provide the support you need now. Outgoing
people with open minds will encourage you to be
yourself and broaden your horizons. Do not be talked
into a situation that will ultimately be unfair or more of
a commitment than you can manage.

Tuesday 22nd

The Sun moves into your money sector today, so your
finances should improve. Remember that Mercury is
still in this area, and he is taking a good look at what
has previously worked and may work again now. Small
business ventures will enhance your bank balance and
allow you some luxuries.

Wednesday 23rd

You may feel flashes of a guilty conscience today. This is most likely down to Mercury, and his exploration into your area of money and shared resources. He is in a connection with Saturn, the teacher, who will try to rein him in. This is a good thing, as Mercury can sometimes become over-enthusiastic in his pursuits.

Thursday 24th

There may be a clash today between you and someone you find grating. You may well be the one who acts with needless aggression, despite the other person sounding off or saying something upsetting. Neither of you can win this dispute, so try to find a resolution together.

Friday 25th

Your creative sector will come into focus today. There are a lot of big ideas that have been on hold, and you want to get them started. There is also a lot to say now. However, you may encounter frustrating restrictions or people trying to silence you.

Saturday 26th

This is the time to check in with your health again. Look at different ways to shake things up a little in your daily routines. You are getting bored and want to inject new enthusiasm into work. Meet up with friends and brainstorm some ideas together.

Sunday 27th

Mercury moves into your communications sector today, where he will increase your desire for meaningful conversations. You will meet people who can satisfy your need to communicate about deep, dark and possibly taboo subjects. Connecting with a brand-new tribe is possible now.

Monday 28th

Today is made for love and the important people in your life. You may feel a desire to merge with another person or with the divine. You may be more empathic now and boundaries can be dissolved. This is not always a good thing. Keep your wits about you.

Tuesday 29th

Saturn turns direct today, and any lessons learnt in your creative sector will now be rewarded. This has been a difficult and restrictive time, but now things are moving forwards again. Venus and Mars have a pleasant connection, which indicates that this is a great day for love. Be brave and ask for what you desire.

Wednesday 30th

You may feel as though you cannot do anything right today. You will most likely have to curb your tenacity and put the brakes on for a while. Elsewhere, a romantic Moon gets creative with the big planets and receives a blessing of bounty. Make the most of it.

OCTOBER

....

Thursday 1st

October begins with a Full Moon. This will illuminate areas in your life where you have been trying to create endings and new beginnings. Subjects you find uncomfortable to think about are at the forefront now, but you know that there is a need to make a decision. What will you do?

Friday 2nd

Venus enters Virgo today, helping to bring beauty and harmony to your outward appearance. You may change your hair colour or buy a new outfit. Elsewhere, you may attract more people into your life, and be able to persuade and coerce them to get what you want.

Saturday 3rd

You can afford a little luxury today. Spend on good food or something new for your home. There is a fantastic energy now that you should make the most of. Feeling good, looking good and fulfilling your needs are the themes of the day.

Sunday 4th

You should be prepared for some emotional baggage to find its way to the surface today. There may be some conversations about past issues that rise up and shock your foundations. You could be left feeling unstable. Deal with what comes up and do not push it back down.

Monday 5th

A positive energy will return today, as all three planets in your creative sector are now direct. This bodes well for falling in love, self-expression and art projects. Children will also feature, and laughter, play and joy return to this area for you. You can aim high and succeed now.

Tuesday 6th

Put your energy into work today. Working on a project with a partner could be satisfying, and you may see solutions where others cannot. Your ability to look at things from all angles will benefit your career and make for a productive day. Check all the small details.

Wednesday 7th

Mercury and Uranus are facing each other in your communications and travel sectors today, which means you may be able to easily discuss unusual subjects or to surprise people. This connection could also mean that somebody will speak unwanted words and cause upsets and disagreements. Do not be that person.

Thursday 8th

Phone a friend or ask the audience. Advice from your social network will be soothing today. Home comforts and motherly love can be acquired from friendship circles. Spend time with close friends who understand your needs and make you feel at home. Those who know you best will welcome your presence.

Friday 9th

There could be a confrontation today, owing to the warrior and power energy being generated by Mars and Pluto. With Mars sitting in your sex sector and Pluto in your love sector, this dispute could take place in one of your key relationships. Venus, in your area of self, can lend the love to soothe the situation.

Saturday 10th

You may not be able to find the energy for creative pursuits today. Instead, you may just want to spend time with friends or on social media. Watch out for someone trying to rock the boat and cause unrest. This could hurt deeply, so it is best avoided. Lie low.

Sunday 11th

There is a restless urge to do something but also do nothing today. You cannot settle on a task or think clearly. Hide yourself away and enjoy a film and some ice cream. Taking the time to relax and be alone will help guide you through this anxious energy.

Monday 12th

Today is best spent focusing on where you are, at this moment. Your mind could be pulled into thoughts of the past and unfinished business. Practise mindfulness and observe where your thoughts are leading without acting on any of them. There is no point dwelling on the past.

Tuesday 13th

The Moon comes into Virgo today, which will help you to review how you serve your community. What do you do out of love? What do you do out of duty? You can be a guiding light for others when you are on top form. Others appreciate your wisdom.

Wednesday 14th

Mercury begins another retrograde period today, and he does so in your communication sector. Review recent conversations or investigations into subjects that you became interested in. Are they working out for you? Transform recent findings into something more useful. Make return visits to newly discovered places.

Thursday 15th

You must look at your finances today. Is there something that you can buy, sell or even invest in? This could be a recent investment that no longer looks like a good deal. Note it, but do not do anything about it until after Mercury retrograde.

Friday 16th

Today, you have a New Moon in your finance sector. This sector also deals with your home and possessions. If there is a home improvement project you have been thinking about, now is the time to put plans into action. You may also be considering sharing your home with another person.

Saturday 17th

This could be a day filled with words. The Moon is making connections to Mercury and Uranus, which suggests that words expressed verbally may come out unfiltered. You may say something that you later regret. Try to use this energy for written words instead. Read and research interesting subjects.

Sunday 18th

A lesson is waiting for you today. Some light is shed on your creative sector that requires attention. You can manage this with great compassion, and this will benefit all involved. This lesson is sent by Saturn, so you had best learn it thoroughly.

Monday 19th

A matter of the heart or project that you are passionate about will get a dual hit today from Venus and Mars. Venus will put her heart and soul into it, but Mars wants to destroy it and forget about it. Whichever way you act, it will be on a Jupiter-sized scale.

Tuesday 20th

Stop digging up the past. You may be like a dog with a bone right now, and will not let something go. It could be playing on your mind and tugging at your heart. Leave it alone. This will ultimately cause chaos, so put it down and step away.

Wednesday 21st

You will be able to get some measure of control back today. You have found what you want, filed it away and are now researching what you are going to do about it. Yesterday's extreme emotions have calmed down. There is gold in what you have found. Hold on to it safely.

Thursday 22nd

There is still a lot of tension in the air, but you will have to get used to it. The Sun has now entered your communications sector, and is heating up the already-hot topics you love so much. You might have to bring something to a close.

Friday 23rd

Health checks are needed now. You may be emotionally drained, and this will affect your physical wellbeing. Mercury retrograde is making himself heard and may have already upset your daily routines. Slow down or step back. You need to look after yourself first and foremost.

Saturday 24th

Venus is in your area of self today, and is pleading with
Saturn to go easy on you. You are sometimes too hard
on yourself and can feel guilty about wasting time, but
you shouldn't worry. Instead, review and assess your
personal boundaries. You cannot be there for everyone.

Sunday 25th

Mercury is in the full heat of the Sun today, in your
communications sector. You may want to let off some
steam. Be warned, Mercury is still retrograde and you
are likely to cause or get involved in arguments. Watch
out for someone trying to fool you.

Monday 26th

The Moon is in your relationship sector, and is making
great connections for a lovely time with a special person.
You can relate well with surprising ease. This can be a
pleasant time and a little respite from Mercury's antics.
Go and do something sweet with a loved one.

Tuesday 27th

Today, you can drift off nicely into fantasy lands with
a partner or close friend. Talking about shared dreams
and visions could be a fun activity. Lovers will want to
merge and singletons will desire a spiritual connection.
Meditation or prayer will nourish your soul.

Wednesday 28th

Venus enters your money sector today, alongside retrograde Mercury. You now have two personal planets bookending this sector. Venus is in her home sign, so she will bring her gifts of money, harmony and self-worth. Mercury wants to take a deeper dive and review these issues.

Thursday 29th

The Moon meets Mars in your sex, death and rebirth sector today. He is still slowly retrograding here, and this is why you haven't felt any progress in this area. End something now. This is a reminder from the Moon that it will be an emotional loss.

Friday 30th

Travel and adventure are now on your mind. You are eager to move on and explore somewhere new, but concrete plans keep crumbling. Maybe this is just not meant for you right now. Take a look at something closer to home like higher education. Learn a new language.

Saturday 31st

Today is a Blue Moon day, which means it is a second Full Moon in one calendar month. This occurs in your travel sector and right on top of Uranus, the disruptor. Make a wish and see what needs to change. This is the right time to let something go.

NOVEMBER

....

Sunday 1st

You are still reeling from yesterday's Full Moon. However, the Moon has moved on and is making a great connection to Jupiter in your creative sector. You will feel emotionally attached to large new projects and will be feeling very positive about them. Lucky Jupiter is on your side.

Monday 2nd

You will be thinking about your career today. Contemplate how far you have come, or not. Is this your vocation at all? Is this right for you? The voice of conscience is likely to tell you to concentrate and get on with it.

Tuesday 3rd

This could be a very harmonious day, as the Moon is holding both Venus and Mars in a friendly embrace. Encounters with the opposite sex will go smoothly, especially workplace connections between male and female colleagues. Equality is the theme of the day.

Wednesday 4th

Mercury finishes his retrograde today, and will go back over the last section of your money area. This may leave you pondering financial commitments or contracts that need to be signed. Anything you may have reviewed in this area will now come back up to be dealt with, once and for all.

Thursday 5th

Now is the time when you want to see your friends and feel like part of a tribe who know you well. You may want to put money into joint investments or spend on a big night out with your social groups. This is not a good idea. Resist the urge to spend too much.

Friday 6th

Plans for a group holiday or expedition may begin to take shape today. However, they will not go smoothly as this travel will eventually be disrupted in some way. Social network groups could become aggressive and you may see some online fighting. Do your very best to remain neutral.

Saturday 7th

Take this weekend for yourself. The Moon in your dreaming sector brings restlessness or laziness. Either way, you will not be very good company. You may be pacing the floor wondering what to do, and become a bear with a sore head when you can't decide.

Sunday 8th

The energy today is stuck and unmoving. As it is a Sunday, this does not matter too much. You may become irritable and attempt to do different chores, but nothing will actually be completed. Getting stuck into a good book is the best thing you can do.

Monday 9th

There will be disharmony between men and women today. This could also be about money that is yours versus money or financial commitments that you share with another. Power struggles and control issues will unsettle you now.

Tuesday 10th

The Moon is in your sign of self today, meaning every little sleight will be felt sharply and be taken personally. There is tension in the air that you cannot deal with. Mercury is in the last degree of your money sector and is urging you to tie up any unfinished business.

Wednesday 11th

Today is buoyant and lively. Expressing your needs and being your unique self comes easily. Get on with any creative projects or things that you are passionate about now. If you show people what you are made of, you cannot fail.

Thursday 12th

The Moon and Venus are sitting together in your money and home sector today. You will delight in this environment and enjoy being in your own space. Money may come in or be spent well. Big changes are going on in your creative sector and these will bring big benefits.

Friday 13th

Today, you are likely to have the type of conversations that most people are afraid of. Research and education can be about esoteric subjects. How might you transform a passion into something that will bring you greater status? This is your time to shine.

Saturday 14th

Mars finally goes direct in your sex, death and rebirth sector. Now is the time to make those big changes and clear the decks for something new to come in. You may be backtracking on a decision made earlier this year that has not gone as expected.

Sunday 15th

Today's New Moon in your communications sector will allow you to investigate deeper topics. There is an urge to learn something new, but this could be something related to your past. Now is the time to dig for gold in your psyche and bring it to the forefront to work on.

Monday 16th

Be careful with financing your new interests today, as your passion and enthusiasm may translate into overspending. Venus is trying to rein you in before it gets out of hand. Jupiter is involved here too, which means that any debts could become unmanageable.

Tuesday 17th

This is one of those days where you must put your money where your mouth is or remain silent. Shock revelations, secrets or talking about taboo subjects will not reflect well on you. More positively, this influence may make you a more inventive and original thinker.

Wednesday 18th

Mars is eager to pick up speed in your sex, death and rebirth sector today but is being held back. This is because his forwards motion is often coupled with aggression and force. March onwards with love, and be mindful of others. Is there something you need to complete?

Thursday 19th

There is a lesson to be learnt today in your communications sector. You may be attending a class or lecture to learn about a topic that is regarded as unusual. Throw your heart into your creative work, and watch the fascinating results. This is a very interesting day for you.

Friday 20th

Right now, daily routines need attention. This may annoy you, as they no longer have the same appeal as new things in your life. This will make you feel burdened and chained. You may well throw a tantrum in an attempt to get your own way.

Saturday 21st

Two planets shift signs today. The Sun is moving into your family sector, bringing back the warmth and laughter of your loved ones. Venus is entering your communications sector, lending harmony and beauty to conversations and intellectual interests. You will find the gold that you went searching for recently.

Sunday 22nd

This is a wonderful day for being with a special person. The Moon is entering your relationship area, allowing you to switch off and enjoy couple time. This could also be a great opportunity to connect with your spirit, so practise yoga, meditation or just have a peaceful time. Enjoy this energy.

Monday 23rd

The Moon is sitting right on top of Neptune today, and it may feel as though you have been washed away to a tropical island. This energy could also mean that you will become lost in the deep blue sea. Keep one foot on solid ground. Fantasy and illusion can be intoxicating.

Tuesday 24th

Mercury may save you from drowning in thoughts today with his incessant questions. You want to know the whys and wherefores of life and death. Slow down and swim to the shore. The answers will not be found in a sea of words. Ground and centre yourself first.

Wednesday 25th

You are eager to get on with exploring the greater mysteries of life. Recent dreaminess now has more common sense, and you will be able to follow paths on solid ground. You will become increasingly motivated, and full of ideas and places you would like to conquer.

Thursday 26th

Your drive and energy will get a boost from hot-headed Mars today, and you may feel more focused than before. However, be careful not to accompany this with Mars' tendency to be aggressive. You have the willpower to start projects but may lose interest in them quickly.

Friday 27th

Venus, the planet of love and money, is opposite Uranus, the planet of disruption, today. These are both in sectors to do with money and travel. Be warned that this could mean arguments or unrest in these areas. A compromise is needed. If you cannot do this, find a way to transmute the tension.

Saturday 28th

A grounded Moon in your travel sector may make you
somewhat unmoving and stubborn today. The Moon is
connecting to Neptune in your relationship sector, who
may want to deceive you. Do not let the wool be pulled
over your eyes. Stay alert for anything or anyone that
does not feel real.

Sunday 29th

There will be a lot of conversation today, and you
may lose your voice. This energy also means that
someone else may be doing all the talking and getting
on your nerves. Someone could even be boasting or
exaggerating. Egos could become inflated now, so keep
yours under control.

Monday 30th

Today is a Full Moon and partial lunar eclipse in your
career sector. There may be unorthodox dealings going
on under the eclipse shadow. Is there someone who is
not playing fair at work? You may learn something today
about boundaries and where they have been crossed.

DECEMBER

....

Tuesday 1st

Mercury is entering your family sector today. As the build-up to the festive season is here, Mercury can be an ally in making plans with family. This time of year can also bring tension with loved ones, so use Mercury's energy well and make sure that everyone is on the same page.

Wednesday 2nd

There may be some early celebrations with friends today. You feel more comfortable with them than with family. They nurture you, or perhaps it is you who is nurturing them? You may feel irritable or vulnerable at this time. A friendly embrace is sure to put it right.

Thursday 3rd

You may feel moody today and vent your irritability on, or with, friends. Part of you wants to leave a situation or get a new one started but you do not have the support to do so. This is just a passing Moon phase, so do not act on it.

Friday 4th

Time alone is the best medicine now. You may feel like a caged animal pacing up and down. When the Moon is in your dream sector, as it is today, you often feel restless. Are you doubting yourself? Take the day or evening to relax.

Saturday 5th

Your restlessness will mutate into immobility today. Emotionally, you want to erupt like a volcano but are keeping it all bubbling under the surface. Let it go or do something productive with it, such as painting or baking. Alternatively, use today to spritz the house ready for the festive season.

Sunday 6th

There will be a lovely connection between Venus and Neptune today, which is great for romance and connecting with a partner. Heads and hearts can be aligned now. Relationships are harmonious. The Moon will move into Virgo this evening, adding to the warm atmosphere.

Monday 7th

Be prepared for a nice surprise today. This could be an early Christmas gift. There is also the potential to surprise yourself too. You may feel or do something that is unusual for you. This is a hidden side but it needs to be shown because it is really very nice.

Tuesday 8th

You may have more passion for creative projects now. If there is anything you want to say, it will be well received. This is a super energy, and you need to roll with it and allow it to expand your chest with pride. Remember to give yourself a clap for something well done.

Wednesday 9th

You may need to organise things around the home today, and your house may benefit from a bit of feng shui. There will be communication with family members, but be wary of being dragged into something that you do not want to do. What looks like a good idea might not be.

Thursday 10th

The fog is shifting from a difficult situation today. This is not a big issue, but it may involve some manipulation. Beware of seductive talk that could lead you astray. Venus, who is in your communications sector, is embracing Pluto in your love and creative sector.

Friday 11th

You will get an energetic boost today, helping you to march into muddier ground. You want to get to the bottom of an issue, excavate it and see what it is all about. Do you really want to be dragging up the past now? Is this a good idea? Think before you act.

Saturday 12th

The Moon is meeting Venus in your communications sector today, where they can talk about the mysteries of life and death. They are likely to tell each other secrets but these may not be theirs to share. Beware of gossipers, and do not be the one spilling the beans about another.

Sunday 13th

A family gathering could be fun today, and you will enjoy the company of outgoing people with an enthusiasm for travel. People interested in higher education will also interest you. This could be a time for telling stories around the campfire. Have fun and let everyone take a turn.

Monday 14th

Today brings a fiery New Moon in your family sector. This Moon also sits with Mercury on a point that is about the past. You can expect a lot of reminiscing about your ancestors' paths. Who are the pioneers in your family? How can you likewise move on?

Tuesday 15th

Venus is gliding into your family sector today, after making an exciting connection with Jupiter. This will infuse love, beauty and harmony into your family relations right on time for the festive celebrations. You may feel enthusiastic and lively now. Travel plans are on your mind, and you may research new places to visit.

Wednesday 16th

Today, your heart may tell you that there is something out there for you that is pure gold. However, it will come with a price. You may chase dreams and manifest them into realities, but there is something you need to let go or transform first. Do not let this opportunity slip by.

Thursday 17th

There is a sense of Alice in Wonderland in the air today. The Moon is visiting Jupiter, which will leave you feeling swollen with joy. Later, the Moon will also meet the great teacher Saturn, and you will feel small again. This could feel very surreal.

Friday 18th

Saturn is moving into your health and duties sector today, and will stay here for the next two-and-a-half years. There will be huge lessons to learn now. Saturn is about boundaries, so you will need to consider where your limits are in what you do for others. Prime health is important now.

Saturday 19th

Jupiter is at the final degree of your love and creativity sector today, lending a sense of urgency and anticipation to the air. Finalise something big and important in this area. You may feel romantic and could make a grand, last-minute gesture.

Sunday 20th

There is a frantic energy today that could feel like a push-and-pull exercise regime. This is the result of Jupiter and Saturn sitting together in your health and duties area. The best thing you can do is go to the gym or do some fitness training. Push, pull and breathe.

Monday 21st

The longest and darkest night is here. The winter solstice marks the Sun and Mercury moving into your love and creativity sector. This can herald cosy nights with a lot of talking. How do you like the thought of being locked away for winter to make beautiful art or poetry?

Tuesday 22nd

You may get a little too close for comfort with someone today. You or another will be digging for secrets or wanting to take a relationship further. This could be as simple as planning a holiday together, but you may not be ready for that. Intimacy could be unwanted now.

Wednesday 23rd

The tension is rising just before the celebrations. There may be issues of aggression and control, which you will feel deeply. People around you will fight for the right to be in charge of the festivities. Let them carry on. Stick to your guns and do not get involved.

Thursday 24th

Yesterday's tensions may now make you want to run away, but this is not possible. This makes you feel very uncomfortable. You may feel resentful over the hold someone has over you. Do some grounding exercises and hold on tight. This could be a bumpy ride.

Friday 25th

Merry Christmas! You might have to put on a festive front today. Volatile emotions will be bumping around as the Moon settles on disruptive Uranus. Speech may be unfiltered and come out with no regard for the consequences. You will feel duty-bound to see the celebrations out before making your escape.

Saturday 26th

Today is much quieter as people have withdrawn to lick their wounds. Fathers and sons are implicated in the recent tension but mothers step in now as peacemakers. There may well be an illusion of peace thrown over the whole day.

Sunday 27th

If you have brought any work home for the break, now is the time to do it. You need to retreat and take your mind off of Christmas. Getting absorbed in filing, statistics, analysis or something similar will make you feel like you again, if only for a few hours.

Monday 28th

You will need to keep family at arm's length today. Venus is doing her best to bring back harmony, but an opposing Moon is making everyone moody. Bridges are being built and bumpy roads are being smoothed over but this is not an easy task. If you were responsible, own it and repair it.

Tuesday 29th

A Full Moon in the sign that rules mothers means that you will need to take care of those who have been hurt. If you are the injured party, take refuge with friends or online groups. This Moon will illuminate the problems that need healing now.

Wednesday 30th

Your thoughts and feelings are not in sync today, so it
is best to keep them to yourself. There are still some
illusions, or possibly even outright lies around you. You
feel like switching off and retreating. This is absolutely
fine. Take it easy.

Thursday 31st

New Year's Eve could be an anticlimax this year. Issues
could get out of hand, so you must stay alert tonight.
Struggles with men may happen, while women may seem
to want to live in the past. Be the better person, and go
into 2021 with an abundance of compassion for everyone.

Virgo

....

PEOPLE WHO
SHARE YOUR SIGN

PEOPLE WHO SHARE YOUR SIGN

. . . .

The valuable influence of warm and hard-working
Virgoans can be felt in the smallest and largest of ways,
from helping just one friend to serving the masses.
From perfectionist performers such as Beyoncé to
Nobel Peace Prize winners such as Mother Teresa,
Virgoans have the capacity to guide and inspire.
Discover the public figures who share your exact
birthday and see if you can spot the similarities.

August 24th

Rupert Grint (1988), Chad Michael Murray (1981), John Green (1977), Alex O'Loughlin (1976), Dave Chappelle (1973), Marlee Matlin (1965), Stephen Fry (1957), Ken Todd (1957), Vince McMahon (1945)

August 25th

Blake Lively (1987), Rachel Bilson (1981), Alexander Skarsgård (1976), Ben Falcone (1973), Claudia Schiffer (1970), Billy Ray Cyrus (1961), Tim Burton (1958), Gene Simmons (1949), Sean Connery (1930), Faustina Kowalska (1905)

August 26th

Keke Palmer (1993), Dylan O'Brien (1991), James Harden (1989), Evan Ross (1988), Macaulay Culkin (1980), Chris Pine (1980), Amanda Schull (1978), Melissa McCarthy (1970), Mother Teresa (1910)

August 27th

Alexa Vega (1988), Patrick J. Adams (1981), Aaron Paul (1979), Suranne Jones (1978), Sarah Chalke (1976), Mark Webber (1976), Tom Ford (1961), Peter Stormare (1953), Paul Reubens (1952), Barbara Bach (1947), U.S. President Lyndon B. Johnson (1908)

August 28th

Armie Hammer (1986), Florence Welch (1986), LeAnn Rimes (1982), Jack Black (1969), Sheryl Sandberg (1969), Shania Twain (1965), David Fincher (1962), Jennifer Coolidge (1961)

August 29th

Liam Payne (1993), Lea Michele (1986), Carla Gugino (1971), Lenny Henry (1958), Temple Grandin (1947), James Hunt (1947), Iris Apfel (1921), Ingrid Bergman (1915)

August 30th

Trevor Jackson (1996), Bebe Rexha (1989), Johanna Braddy (1987), Cameron Diaz (1972), Michael Chiklis (1963), Warren Buffett (1930), Ernest Rutherford (1871)

August 31st

Sara Ramirez (1975), Chris Tucker (1971), Queen Rania of Jordan (1970), Tsai Ing-wen, President of the Republic of China (1956), Marcia Clark (1953), Richard Gere (1949), Van Morrison (1945), Georg Jensen (1866)

September 1st

Zendaya (1996), Daniel Sturridge (1989), Chanel West Coast (1988), Boyd Holbrook (1981), Gloria Estefan (1957), Phil McGraw aka Dr Phil (1950), Barry Gibb (1946), Lily Tomlin (1939)

September 2nd

Alexandre Pato (1989), Zedd (1989), Salma Hayek (1966), Lennox Lewis (1965), Keanu Reeves (1964), Eugenio Derbez (1961), Mark Harmon (1951), Robert Shapiro (1942)

September 3rd

Kaia Gerber (2001), Dominic Thiem (1993), Shaun White (1986), Garrett Hedlund (1984), Fearne Cotton (1981), Redfoo (1975), Charlie Sheen (1965), Malcolm Gladwell (1963), Jaggi Vasudev (1957)

September 4th

Yannick Carrasco (1993), James Bay (1990), Beyoncé (1981), Max Greenfield (1980), Wes Bentley (1978), Mark Ronson (1975), Damon Wayans (1960), Drew Pinsky aka Dr Drew (1958)

September 5th

Giovanni Pernice (1990), Kat Graham (1989), Annabelle Wallis (1984), Carice van Houten (1976), Rose McGowan (1973), Michael Keaton (1951), Freddie Mercury (1946), Raquel Welch (1940), Jesse James (1847)

September 6th

Lauren Lapkus (1985), Pippa Middleton (1983), Kerry Katona (1980), Naomie Harris (1976), Idris Elba (1972), Anika Noni Rose (1972), Macy Gray (1967), Swoosie Kurtz (1944), Roger Waters (1943), Jane Addams (1860)

September 7th

Evan Rachel Wood (1987), Oliver Hudson (1976), Shannon Elizabeth (1973), Leslie Jones (1967), Toby Jones (1966), Eazy-E (1964), Gloria Gaynor (1949), Buddy Holly (1936)

September 8th

Cameron Dallas (1994), Joe Sugg (1991), Avicii (1989), Wiz Khalifa (1987), P!nk (1979), David Arquette (1971), Martin Freeman (1971), Bernie Sanders (1941), Antonín Dvořák (1841)

September 9th

Luka Modrić (1985), Zoe Kazan (1983), Michelle Williams (1980), Michael Bublé (1975), Adam Sandler (1966), Hugh Grant (1960), Colonel Sanders (1890), Leo Tolstoy (1828)

September 10th

Ryan Phillippe (1974), Guy Ritchie (1968), Jack Ma (1964), Colin Firth (1960), Joe Perry (1950), Bill O'Reilly (1949), Mary Oliver (1935), Karl Lagerfeld (1933), Cynthia Lennon (1939)

September 11th

Kygo (1991), Tyler Hoechlin (1987), Ludacris (1977), Taraji P. Henson (1970), Harry Connick Jr. (1967), Moby (1965), Scott Patterson (1958)

September 12th

Connor Franta (1992), Alfie Allen (1986), Emmy Rossum (1986), Jennifer Hudson (1981), Ben McKenzie (1979), Paul Walker (1973), Hans Zimmer (1957), Barry White (1944), Jesse Owens (1913)

September 13th

Niall Horan (1993), Ben Savage (1980), Fabio Cannavaro (1973), Stella McCartney (1971), Tyler Perry (1969), Dave Mustaine (1961), Jacqueline Bisset (1944), Roald Dahl (1916)

September 14th

Jessica Brown Findlay (1989), Amy Winehouse (1983), Ben Cohen (1978), Andrew Lincoln (1973), Nas (1973), Sam Neill (1947), Margaret Sanger (1879)

September 15th

Poppy Delevingne (1986), Jenna Marbles (1986), Prince Harry, Duke of Sussex (1984), Tom Hardy (1977), Jimmy Carr (1972), Queen Letizia of Spain (1972), Tommy Lee Jones (1946), Agatha Christie (1890), U.S. President William Howard Taft (1857)

September 16th

Nick Jonas (1992), Alexis Bledel (1981), Flo Rida (1979), Amy Poehler (1971), Marc Anthony (1968), Molly Shannon (1964), Mickey Rourke (1952), Peter Falk (1927), B.B. King (1925), Lauren Bacall (1924)

September 17th

Anastacia (1968), Cheryl Strayed (1968), Kyle Chandler (1965), Narendra Modi, 14th Prime Minister of India (1950), John Ritter (1948), Jim Rohn (1930), Hank Williams (1923), Billy the Kid (1859), Melissa Hemsley (1985)

September 18th

Patrick Schwarzenegger (1993), Jason Sudeikis (1975), Xzibit (1974), James Marsden (1973), Jada Pinkett Smith (1971), Aisha Tyler (1970), James Gandolfini (1961), John McAfee (1945)

September 19th

Danielle Panabaker (1987), Lauren Goodger (1986), Skepta (1982), Jimmy Fallon (1974), Sanaa Lathan (1971), Lita Ford (1958), Twiggy (1949), Jeremy Irons (1948), Adam West (1928)

September 20th

Phillip Phillips (1990), Jon Bernthal (1976), Victor Ponta, Former Prime Minister of Romania (1972), Michelle Visage (1968), Kristen Johnston (1967), George R. R. Martin (1948), Sophia Loren (1934), Anne Meara (1929), Upton Sinclair (1878)

September 21st

Jason Derulo (1989), Maggie Grace (1983), Nicole Richie (1981), Liam Gallagher (1972), Alfonso Ribeiro (1971), Luke Wilson (1971), Faith Hill (1967), Abby Lee Miller (1966), Shinzō Abe, 63rd Prime Minister of Japan (1954), Bill Murray (1950), Stephen King (1947), Leonard Cohen (1934)

September 22nd

Daniela Ospina (1992), Tom Felton (1987), Thiago Silva (1984), Billie Piper (1982), Ronaldo (1976), Sue Perkins (1969), Andrea Bocelli (1958), Joan Jett (1958), Nick Cave (1957), Rosamunde Pilcher (1924)

September 23rd

Anthony Mackie (1978), Karl Pilkington (1972), Jason Alexander (1959), Bruce Springsteen (1949), Julio Iglesias (1943), Romy Schneider (1938), Ray Charles (1930), Mickey Rooney (1920)